Dear Fellow Investor—

Would you like to know how you could be on the right side of every trade?

Have you been burned trying to pick the top or bottom of a stock or ETF?

Would you like to spend less time analyzing and more time enjoying life?

It's time to stop giving the market permission to steal your peace, and hard-earned money. You will discover for yourself how to produce amazing, consistent, and reliable investment results year after year.

If you find yourself nodding in agreement . . . I know exactly how you feel. You intuitively know there is a better way, but you're not sure where to start or who to trust.

Well, if I could look you in the eye I would say—your search is over! In this book I reveal a very unique system designed with you in mind . . . one that will guide you effortlessly how to grow wealthy.

Contrary to popular belief, the biggest threat to your wealth is the age-old idea of "buy and hold" investing. Millions of investors, possibly you included, have fallen prey to this antiquated, failed system and have lost tens of thousands of hard-earned dollars.

I want every investor to be on the right side of every trade. Yes the proprietary algorithms behind my system are complex, but I've made it so easy for you to use.

Just click a few buttons and the computer goes to work crunching all the numbers. Within a few minutes you have a guide for a list of stocks and ETF's.

Even with all the fundamental analysis, price earnings ratios, economic projections, news events, pundits on TV, all they tell you is where they "think the market should be." Just remember that nothing matters but price.

It's actually true that the market will tell you what it's going to do next. That's right, the market will tell you everything you need to know, you just need to learn how to listen, and I'm about to show you how.

Does history repeat itself? Some say yes, some say no, others say everything is random.

My position, based on over twenty-five years of investing experience, is that the stock market is not random and that history does repeat itself. The key to investing success is to recognize this and take advantage of it, which I have done very successfully.

By knowing what to look for and observing just a few of the signals on any given stock or ETF you can catch the biggest and most profitable market swings.

The incredible breakthrough I've been talking about is called the VISIONS VTAM Black Box. It is a member of the VISIONS investor tool set that has made investors like you a lot of money. If you are able to predict the direction of a stock with a high degree of accuracy, then the opportunity for success is endless. That is what I am revealing to you in this book.

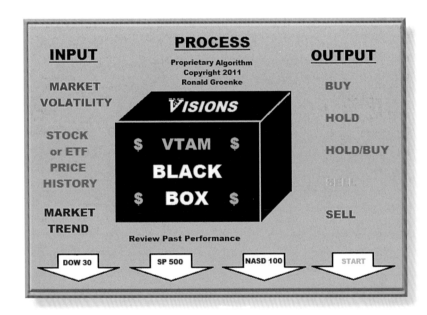

VISIONS VTAM (Groenke V Technical Analysis Model) implements a Black Box algorithm that looks at what has happened in the past for any stock or ETF and provides an indication of when to Buy, Hold, Sell, or just Wait (do nothing). The details of the algorithm are revealed and described for your review and analysis.

Don't risk your family's future to a guess, hunch, hope, or intuition. When the signal says wait...then wait. When it says buy . . . then buy. When it says sell . . . then sell. When the signal is unclear . . . then sit on your hands and do nothing, or write covered calls against your existing positions to generate some additional cash flow (I teach you how in the chapters which follow).

The recession of 2008 to 2010 is well understood. Most stocks were down and went nowhere during this period except for a few like Apple stock (AAPL). With the signals from the VISIONS VTAM Black Box you could have taken a generous return to the bank, as your take would have been over 100%. If you had invested in General Electric (GE) your take would have been over 85%. This is the time frame where GE was up and down and ended flat for the period. Further details are provided in the chapters that follow.

The strategy behind VISIONS tells you when to take the gains to the bank. And best of all you can use it free for 21 days to see how it will work to improve your own portfolio. During this free trial, many trial users have made enough to pay for all of their future licenses. You have nothing to lose and a lot to gain.

If the returns on your investments seem unreal after you have applied the techniques provided here that's great news for you. You keep the rewards of your new investment skills and I have the satisfaction knowing that I was able to help advance your financial success.

Happy investing,
Ron Groenke

Visit my website—www.RonGroenke.com—for additional information.

Other Books by Ronald Groenke

The Money Tree: Risk Free Options Trading (2002)

Covered Calls and Naked Puts: Create Your Own Stock Options Money Tree (2004)

Cash For Life: Unlock the Incredible Monthly Cash Income in Your Stock Portfolio (2006)

Show Me the Money: Covered Calls and Naked Puts for a Monthly Cash Income (2009)

Show Me the Trade is the latest book that reveals new concepts and tactics for successful stock market investing.

An important theme in all my books is wise stock selection. After all, if you are going to have an orchard of money trees you want the trees to be as healthy as possible. I've created a unique technique for increasing the odds of *buying low and selling higher.*

My books also teach you how to earn income on your stock portfolio. They provide the concepts and techniques I have practiced over twenty-five years in generating income on my stock holdings.

Detailed formulas and stock and option selection criteria are revealed and discussed.

It is my hope that these techniques, which have served me so well, will also be profitable for you.

A word of caution: Be very deliberate in your investing. Do your homework. Study this book carefully and master the techniques.

You will find my software, which I call VISIONS, to be an important resource. (See Chapter 18 for details). It is the software program that I created and use to find quality stocks and options. It implements the technical analysis techniques explained here to indicate when to Buy and Sell. It also shows Call and Put options with premiums that generate the best returns. This Internet based software takes the drudgery out of surfing the Internet for stock and option information. Spend your time analyzing the potential trades suggested by VISIONS. It puts all the information right at your fingertips.

SHOW ME THE TRADE

Revolutionary **BLACK BOX**
for Profit in Stock and Options

Ronald Groenke

KELLER PUBLISHING
Marco Island, Florida

Paperback ISBN 978-1-934002-76-6
eISBN 978-1-934002-77-3

Published by
Keller Publishing
440 Seaview Ct. Suite 1012
Marco Island, FL 34145

www.KellerPublishing.com

To my beautiful wife Jean,
who has given me many
years of love, support, and
encouragement

Contents

Acknowledgment

Thanks to my wonderful friends Wade and Sue Keller for all their efforts in editing the manuscript and providing the publishing services for all of my books.

I am also very grateful to many of my previous book readers and software users who have provided feedback on how to improve the investment process. They have been an excellent sounding board and provided a base of support in refining the concepts and techniques described in this book. This willingness to share has allowed you to gain a little edge in the investing world. You can do the same by sharing the concepts in this book with your family and friends.

Opportunity Knocks

"An investment in knowledge pays the best interest."
Benjamin Franklin

Are you an investor or a trader? It depends on your point of view. An investor is a person who commits money in order to earn a financial return. A trader is a person whose business is buying and selling regularly. I consider myself an investor that trades equities. I commit assets to generate a return. In the process I buy and sell knowing that to earn a return one needs to sell the asset at a higher price than its purchase price. You make money by selling.

If you buy and hold equity without the intent to sell, perhaps you are a collector. The asset may be worth a lot more in the future, but that could be generations away. If the past ten years is any indication of the future, buy and hold could be termed a collector strategy.

Generating a positive return is possible if you know when to buy and when to sell. Equities have up and down cycles just like the economy. Some equities are in step with the economic cycle and others are not. A great example is Apple. During the last recession (2009–10) when many equities like General Electric (GE) were falling with the economic downturn, other companies like Apple (AAPL) were moving up and making new highs. On the following page you see a four-year history chart of Apple (AAPL) and General Electric (GE). Note the

1

difference: GE has not yet returned to its prior highs of 2007 and AAPL has almost doubled since its 2007 high.

This is the beauty and challenge of investing in equities. If you are able to predict the direction of a stock with a high degree of accuracy, then the opportunity for success is endless. That is what I am revealing to you in this book. My technical analysis algorithm and process uses stock trading history to determine when to buy and sell any stock. To demonstrate my process, let's look at the opportunity to generate a return in AAPL or GE. In looking at the charts it seems rather obvious that one could buy AAPL and just hold it since it is going up (in hind-sight). With GE it is more difficult. But the opportunity with AAPL and GE is almost identical if you know when to buy and sell.

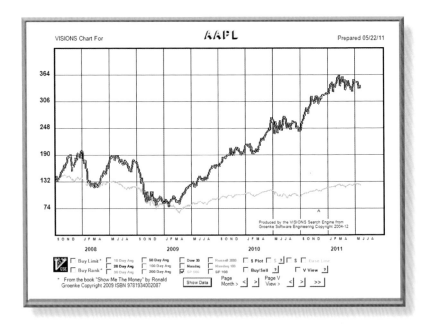

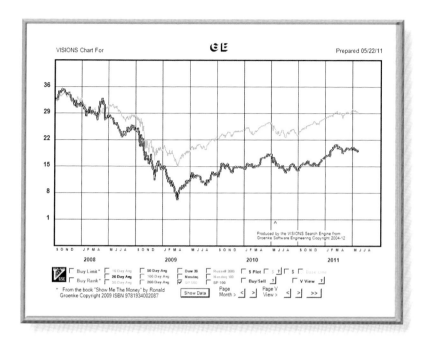

Here are the trades that my process identified over the four-year period for GE. There is a return of over 87%. Not bad for a stock going nowhere.

```
VISIONS Chart Buy/Sell Trade Report for GE on 05/22/11

Buy  on 09/04/07 @ 33.54
Sell on 03/07/08 @ 28.37 for gain of -5.17/Share or -15.41 %

Buy  on 03/11/08 @ 29.40
Sell on 03/24/08 @ 32.92 for gain of 3.52/Share or 11.97 %

Buy  on 07/29/08 @ 25.27
Sell on 09/17/08 @ 20.82 for gain of -4.45/Share or -17.61 %

Buy  on 11/28/08 @ 15.49
Sell on 01/14/09 @ 12.97 for gain of -2.52/Share or -16.27 %

Buy  on 03/13/09 @ 9.10
Sell on 03/27/09 @ 10.20 for gain of 1.10/Share or 12.09 %

Buy  on 03/31/09 @ 9.57
Sell on 04/14/09 @ 10.89 for gain of 1.32/Share or 13.79 %

Buy  on 04/15/09 @ 11.19
Sell on 05/11/09 @ 13.43 for gain of 2.24/Share or 20.02 %

Buy  on 06/25/09 @ 11.31
Sell on 08/10/09 @ 13.90 for gain of 2.59/Share or 22.90 %

Buy  on 08/18/09 @ 12.97
Sell on 09/17/09 @ 15.99 for gain of 3.02/Share or 23.28 %

Buy  on 11/09/09 @ 15.21
Sell on 03/17/10 @ 17.53 for gain of 2.32/Share or 15.25 %

Buy  on 07/23/10 @ 15.37
Sell on 10/14/10 @ 16.91 for gain of 1.54/Share or 10.02 %

Buy  on 11/04/10 @ 16.27
Sell on 12/23/10 @ 17.92 for gain of 1.65/Share or 10.14 %

Buy  on 03/30/11 @ 20.11
Waiting to Sell       Current Gain of -2.44 %

These trades if followed provided a 48 Month Gain of 87.74 %
```

Here are the trades that my process identified over the four-year period for AAPL. Apple has a return of over 109%.

```
VISIONS Chart Buy/Sell Trade Report for AAPL on 05/22/11

Buy  on 09/13/07 @ 137.20
Sell on 10/09/07 @ 167.86 for gain of 30.66/Share or 22.35 %

Buy  on 03/25/08 @ 140.98
Sell on 04/30/08 @ 173.95 for gain of 32.97/Share or 23.39 %

Buy  on 08/12/08 @ 176.73
Sell on 09/04/08 @ 161.22 for gain of -15.51/Share or -8.78 %

Buy  on 01/22/09 @ 88.36
Sell on 03/24/09 @ 106.50 for gain of 18.14/Share or 20.53 %

Buy  on 01/27/10 @ 207.88
Sell on 04/26/10 @ 269.50 for gain of 61.62/Share or 29.64 %

Buy  on 07/20/10 @ 251.89
Sell on 10/19/10 @ 309.49 for gain of 57.60/Share or 22.87 %

Buy  on 04/13/11 @ 336.13
Waiting to Sell        Current Gain of -0.27 %

These trades if followed provided a 48 Month Gain of 109.73 %
```

If you had purchased GE at the beginning of the period (9-4-2007) and sold at the end of the period (5-20-2011) you would have experienced a 41% loss ($13.92 per share). For AAPL the result would be a 132% gain ($191.06 per share).

Now here is where judgment and style of investing enter the picture. I believe it is more productive to take a number of small gains to the bank over time rather than going for the big win. Singles and doubles win a lot of baseball games. Home runs are nice but very unpredictable.

I have experienced this many times during the last twenty-five years of investing. No need to get greedy. You may think you are missing the big one-time gain, but the trade data shows that you can be just as successful with a slow-moving industrial like GE versus a high-flying technology company like Apple.

The chapters, which follow, provide additional detail on an investing concept that optimizes when to buy and sell. A chapter is provided for each type of trading strategy to consider. Sample trades are provided that "Show the Trade" in detail. Actual trades and results are provided in the Walk The Talk chapter. It shows what is possible over a long period of time including the results during the market correction in 2009. Once you understand these concepts and apply them they will improve your financial success.

The examples provided, include the cost of trading (commissions) at a typical discount brokerage firm. The returns shown are net after these costs and try to represent what is possible.

Magical Black Box

"If there is a way to do it better ... find it."

Thomas Edison

Have you heard about computerized or Black Box trading? There is really no mystery involved when you see what I have to show you. My black box discovery will open a new world of stock market success that should satisfy even the biggest skeptic.

The algorithm or step-by-step process described below can be accomplished with a hand calculator, pencil and paper. But unless you are another Albert Einstein, the time required to do all the calculations could be overwhelming. That's a disadvantage. Hedge funds and brokerage houses employ expensive computer technology to get a market advantage.

With a process that can be implemented very nicely on your personal computer, you can get the same or better advantage. I call my discovery VTAM, which stands for (Groenke **V** Technical Analysis Model). It's a Black Box algorithm and process based on a technical analysis concept of an equity Buy Limit and trade history that was previously introduced in my book *Show Me the Money*. I have revised and added functions that optimized the results for any stock or ETF. By following the buy and sell signals defined in my process below, your investing strategy will give you a huge advantage.

The Buy Limit is the price at which you would consider purchasing an equity. It is defined as follows:

Buy Limit = RLow + F x (RHigh – RLow)

Where:

RLow = the Low price for the Range being considered.

RHigh = the High price for the Range being considered.

F = a fraction with a value between of .25 to .50.

Range is the period history of 10 to 52 weeks.

For example, let's look at a 52 week Range Buy Limit.

RLow = 52 week low

RHigh = 52 week high, and

F = .25

Buy Limit = 52 Week Low + .25 x (52 Week High—52 Week Low)

Here is the Buy Limit view for GE with these settings.

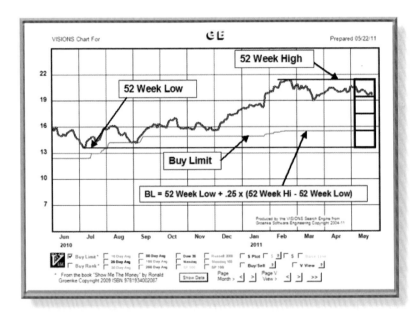

I have drawn what looks like a ladder on the upper right area of the graph. This ladder has four equal steps. The Buy Limit line is drawn by applying this ladder at each daily closing price, and then, placing a point at the one-quarter mark on the ladder. So looking back in time you can see the Buy Limit value. Except for a period in early 2011 this was not a candidate for investment since the stock was trading above the buy limit most of the time.

Now let's change the range to 15 weeks and use a fraction of .50. Here is the new graph.

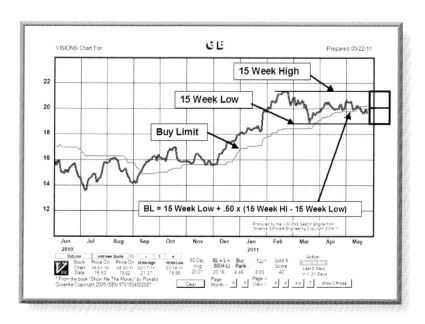

The new ladder has two steps since the fraction is one-half. The Buy Limit has values that provide more opportunities for possible invest-ment. Is this the Buy Limit that provides the optimum return for GE? If we can answer this question we could be on our way to something HUGE.

The first part of technical analysis is the construction of my Groenke **V** for any stock (the **V** part of VTAM). The **V** is formulated to provide a set of boundaries in which a stock may trade. Once a stock starts trading in the V, it may become an opportunity for investment in the near future. These boundaries and the construction of the **V** is based on many years of modeling, analysis, and application with real trades. This has provided the following criteria for its construction.

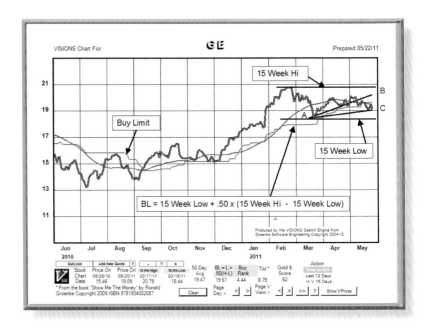

Place a point A at the Low for the range 50 trades back in time. Place a point B at the Buy Limit plus ½ the fraction times the High minus the Low. Place a point C at the Low plus ½ the fraction times the High minus the Low. Now draw a line from A to B and a line from A to C. Here is an example for GE using the Buy Limit with a 15-week High Low range and a .50 fraction.

The **V** is drawn for the last trade date (5-22-11) on the chart. A is at 18.95, B at 20.77 and c at 19.56. The stock is at 19.62 and is currently in the V. If you look back at the last 50 trading days you can count the number of times the stock has traded inside the **V** boundaries, which equals 16. For a stock to stay in the **V** it must be moving up. This is key to determining when it is the appropriate to make an investment in this stock. Here is a closer view.

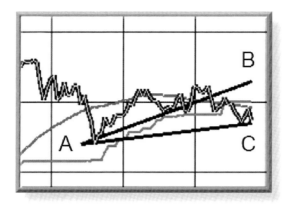

I believe stocks follow well-defined trading cycles that can be used to predict stock trading direction. My numerous years of analysis and experience indicate that a stock price has demonstrated a major new up cycle when:

1) It has traded in the **V** for twenty days or more.
2) Is currently in the **V** or within 5% (plus or minus) of the 50 day moving average.
3) Has traded up the last three days.

The following formula provides a Black Box signal of when to buy.

Gold $ = 10 * (# of up days [3 max])

+ 2 * (# of days in **V** [20 max])

+ 30 or 0 (30 if the price of stock is in the **V**, or within +/-5 % of the 50 day average range, 0 if it not).

A value of 100 indicates an ideal case and that all criteria are met. The ideal case is when:

1) A stock is trading in the **V** for 20 days or more.
2) Is going up the last 3 days.
3) Is in the **V** or within +/– 5% of the 50 day moving average.

Here is the GE graph with Gold $ displayed anytime the value is 71 or greater.

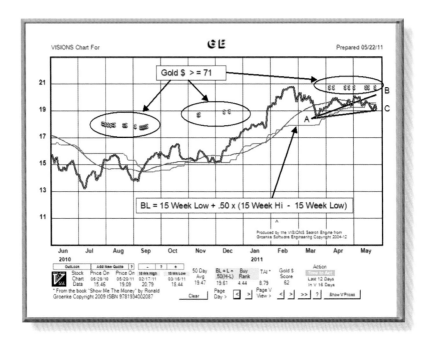

Each Gold $ value greater or equal to 71 indicates when it may be a good time to make an investment in GE. So this is our third variable. The Gold $ is the value that signals when to BUY. This value has a range from 71 to 100. The ideal case is 100. A value of 71 provides a lower bound such that a stock must be in the **V** and trading up.

Now if we know when to BUY, at what point do we SELL? Knowing when to sell is as important as knowing when to buy. Deciding when to sell can be a tough decision. Is the price going higher? Should we sell now or wait?

What if the decision of when to sell was made for you? This is the other half of VTAM Black Box. It provides a SELL signal that maximizes the gains and minimizes the losses. It is an automated by-the-numbers process that removes emotion from the decision.

When to sell has two parts. The first is selling at a gain and the second is selling at a loss. Doing these at the right time will maximize your result. So yes, timing is important. If our model can provide these variables, we should be in a position to maximize our success. These are the fourth and fifth variables in our Black Box algorithm. Sell at a specific percent gain and sell at a specific percent loss.

The following sell criteria are then established.

Sell at a gain when the stock reaches or exceeds the sell price (based on % gain variable) and a down day is experienced. Once we have met our gain criteria it is better to take the gain to the bank than risk further deterioration in the price. This is the **do not get greedy factor** I mentioned many times before. A number of small gains is more productive than going for the grand slam.

Sell at a loss when the price falls below the percent loss criteria.

The five variables of the VTAM Black Box therefore are:

1—Buy Limit High/Low range—value of 10 to 52 weeks
2—Buy Limit Fraction—value of .25 to .50
3—Gold $ When to Buy Signal—value of 71 to 100
4—Sell on Gain—value of 5 to 20 %
5—Sell on Loss—value of 5 to 20%.

You can think of this as a Black Box with five knobs. By turning each knob we get a new result. Running the VTAM Black Box with all possibilities will allow us to determine which combination provides for the maximum return for any stock or ETF for any time period.

For our GE example above lets use 10% for Sell on Gain, and 5% for Sell at Loss.

Here is the graph with Buy and Sell indicated.

These settings provided a 12-month return of 15.25%.
Here are the trades.

```
VISIONS Chart Buy/Sell Trade Report for GE on 5/22/11

Buy Limit Fraction = 0.50 and High/Low Range = 15 weeks.

Buy when number of up days = 3, trading in the Groenke V for 20 days,
 or currently trading in the V, or within +/- 5.0 % of the 50 day
average,
 a VISIONS Chart Gold $ Score that is >= 71.

Sell on upside gain of 10.0 % (after a downturn) or when loss > 5.0 %

These criteria if followed provided a 12 Month Gain of 15.25 %

Buy  on 07/23/10 @ 15.10
Sell on 08/23/10 @ 14.31 for gain of -0.79/Share or -5.23 %

Buy  on 09/02/10 @ 14.56
Sell on 10/11/10 @ 16.42 for gain of 1.86/Share or 12.77 %

Buy  on 11/04/10 @ 15.98
Sell on 12/23/10 @ 17.60 for gain of 1.62/Share or 10.14 %

Buy  on 03/30/11 @ 19.76
Waiting to Sell       Current Gain of -2.43 %
```

Lets review the data to provide a better understanding of what has transpired.

The first Buy signal was on 7/23/10 at $15.10. The stock moved up but did not reach our 10% gain point and then went down. When it was more then 5% down a Sell was indicated on 8/23/10 at $14.31 for a loss of $.79 per share or 5.23%.

The next Buy was signaled on 9/2/10 at $14.56 and a Sell on 10/11/10 for a gain of $1.86 per share or 12.77%. The stock went up to $16.49 but then went back down. It was correct to take the gain to the bank. A Buy was next signaled on 11/4/10 at $15.98 and a Sell on 12/23/10 at $17.60 for a gain of $1.62 per share or 10.14 %.

The last Buy was on 3/30/11 at $19.76 with a waiting to sell condition.

For this 12-month period being reviewed the overall gain was 15.25%. This includes the 2.43% loss at the last price on the chart.

"What about different settings for the sell on gain and sell on loss criteria?" We can run the VTAM Black Box for all the variables and let it tell us the best setting for each variable. These can be used to provide us with a guide of when to Buy and Sell this investment in the future.

Here is the 12-month VTAM Black Box optimum result for GE.

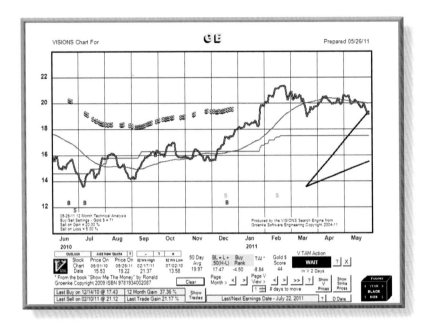

This VTAM Black Box result shows that a 12-month gain of over 37% was possible. Does this really work? Based on feedback for early users of the concept, and my own experience, it does an excellent job. Following the VTAM Black Box indicators has provided investment success over 80% of the time. One way to demonstrate this is to look at various periods and see if the Black Box produces consistent results. To demonstrate this we apply the VTAM Black Box settings to the 24 and 12-month time periods and see if the results provided are acceptable. What is acceptable? Generating a 25% return every year seems practicable and highly acceptable. Here is an example with Hecla Mining (HL).

The VTAM Black Box settings are as follows:

> Buy Limit High/Low range—value of 45 weeks
>
> Buy Limit Fraction—value of .50
>
> Gold $ When to Buy Signal—value of 78
>
> Sell on Gain—value of 20 %
>
> Sell on Loss—value of 5 %

Here is the chart for the 12-month period. Gain was 54.46%.

Here is the chart for the 24-month period. Gain was 126.70%.

You may be a little skeptical about what was presented and might think that maybe I found a specific stock to fit the model. This is not the case. The next chapter shows a number of stocks and ETF's with a 40% or more return in twelve months.

Applying the concept to the DOW 30 stocks produces very acceptable results. Here is the summary that shows significant returns for all 30 stocks over a twelve-month period.

DOW 30 Twelve Month Return Summary
Prepared 6-9-2011

Stock	Action	Gold $ Value	Gold $ Setting	Sell on Gain	Sell on Loss	Week Range	Buy Limit Fraction	12 Month Gain
AA	WAIT	9	78	20	5	52	0.30	49.67
AXP	WAIT	56	73	5	9	10	0.50	48.07
BA	WAIT	44	75	8	5	10	0.30	44.95
PFE	WAIT	30	75	20	5	15	0.35	42.66
GE	WAIT	58	71	20	5	52	0.50	42.57
CVX	HOLD	74	73	20	5	10	0.50	41.93
CAT	HOLD	26	71	20	5	10	0.50	40.95
VZ	WAIT	64	75	10	5	10	0.45	38.37
MMM	HOLD	66	71	9	5	10	0.45	37.09
UTX	WAIT	48	71	6	7	10	0.50	36.86
INTC	WAIT	40	71	7	5	25	0.35	34.32
T	WAIT	40	75	15	5	25	0.35	32.89
DD	WAIT	20	81	15	5	10	0.45	31.51
TRV	WAIT	56	75	6	5	15	0.50	31.05
JPM	WAIT	42	73	7	15	52	0.45	30.94
KO	WAIT	52	71	15	5	10	0.40	30.10
DIS	WAIT	40	75	20	6	45	0.50	29.75
KFT	HOLD	40	71	15	5	25	0.50	27.32
IBM	HOLD	48	71	20	5	15	0.50	27.07
MCD	HOLD	60	78	15	5	15	0.35	26.42
HD	WAIT	9	81	20	5	52	0.30	26.26
CSCO	WAIT	26	81	7	5	15	0.45	25.53
PG	WAIT	34	71	5	5	35	0.50	24.91
MRK	WAIT	60	78	6	5	10	0.50	24.88
XOM	WAIT	40	75	15	5	25	0.30	22.33
BAC	WAIT	30	91	15	5	25	0.30	21.79
JNJ	WAIT	40	71	10	5	30	0.25	21.78
WMT	HOLD	30	73	15	5	52	0.45	21.52
HPQ	WAIT	4	91	15	5	25	0.30	18.06
MSFT	WAIT	48	91	5	5	50	0.25	11.28

Running the VTAM Black Box on all the stocks in the S&P 500 provides over 200 stocks with a twenty-percent or better return per year. Here is the list with returns of 40% or more.

A chart is provided for the stock at the top and bottom of this list to demonstrate the concept.

SP500 Stocks with 40% or Better Twelve-Month Return Summary
Prepared 6-9-2011

Stock	Action	Gold $ Value	Gold $ Setting	Sell on Gain	Sell on Loss	Week Range	Buy Limit Fraction	12 Month Gain
NFLX	WAIT	10	75	20	5	15	0.50	91.69
FTI	WAIT	50	81	20	5	10	0.50	77.29
HAL	BUY	72	71	9	10	10	0.50	59.13
NVDA	HOLD	60	71	20	5	30	0.50	57.12
CRM	HOLD	28	75	20	15	10	0.45	55.76
APOL	HOLD	40	83	20	5	10	0.30	55.74
AMD	WAIT	34	71	5	5	52	0.50	53.70
CMG	HOLD	56	73	20	8	10	0.35	52.87
HUM	WAIT	36	71	20	10	10	0.45	52.28
F	HOLD	60	73	20	5	45	0.50	51.39
MU	WAIT	38	78	20	20	52	0.45	47.59
PCLN	WAIT	54	71	20	15	10	0.40	46.89
RF	WAIT	36	73	5	10	40	0.40	46.70
JBL	WAIT	30	73	20	5	52	0.50	46.37
RDC	WAIT	46	73	20	20	15	0.50	45.92
SNDK	HOLD	48	78	6	6	35	0.50	45.73
BTU	HOLD	64	71	20	6	40	0.50	45.53
EP	WAIT	30	73	5	10	10	0.50	45.46
FFIV	HOLD	36	73	20	9	10	0.50	45.00
BA	WAIT	40	75	8	5	10	0.30	44.95
CF	WAIT	52	73	20	10	10	0.50	44.87
CSX	HOLD	58	71	20	10	10	0.50	44.75
BXP	WAIT	34	73	20	10	10	0.45	44.71
ETFC	SELL	14	71	15	5	10	0.40	44.05
CAT	HOLD	18	73	20	5	10	0.40	43.34
JCP	WAIT	4	78	20	10	10	0.35	43.32
AA	WAIT	9	71	20	15	52	0.45	43.29
RAI	WAIT	38	73	20	5	10	0.45	42.34
CTXS	WAIT	2	71	15	5	10	0.35	42.15
FLS	WAIT	32	71	20	10	52	0.40	42.05
TIF	WAIT	0	78	20	10	52	0.50	41.35
AXP	WAIT	52	71	6	8	10	0.45	41.3
SPG	WAIT	50	73	20	5	10	0.50	40.86
GWW	WAIT	38	71	20	10	10	0.50	40.81
AN	WAIT	70	71	5	15	10	0.50	40.57

VISIONS Chart Buy/Sell Trade Report for NFLX on 06/09/11

Buy Limit Fraction = 0.50 and High/Low Range = 15 weeks.

Buy when number of up days = 3, trading in the Groenke V for 20 days,
currently trading in the V or within +/- 5.0 % of the 50 day average,
and with a VISIONS Chart Gold $ Score that is >= 75.

Sell on upside gain of 20.0 % (after a downturn) or when loss > 5.0 %

These criteria if followed provided a 12 Month Gain of 91.69 %

Buy on 08/05/10 @ 110.53
Sell on 08/17/10 @ 132.97 for gain of 22.44/Share or 20.30 %

Buy on 08/26/10 @ 125.84
Sell on 09/28/10 @ 161.86 for gain of 36.02/Share or 28.62 %

Buy on 01/13/11 @ 191.49
Sell on 02/15/11 @ 240.79 for gain of 49.30/Share or 25.75 %

Buy on 02/24/11 @ 215.18
Sell on 03/02/11 @ 204.23 for gain of -10.95/Share or -5.09 %

Buy on 03/10/11 @ 200.02
Sell on 04/05/11 @ 244.23 for gain of 44.21/Share or 22.10 %

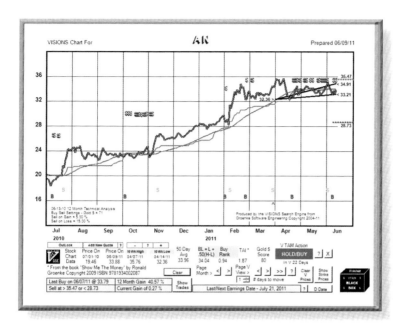

```
VISIONS Chart Buy/Sell Trade Report for AN on 06/09/11

Buy Limit Fraction = 0.50 and High/Low Range = 10 weeks.

Buy when number of up days = 3, trading in the Groenke V for 20 days,
currently trading in the V or within +/- 5.0 % of the 50 day average,
and with a VISIONS Chart Gold $ Score that is >= 71.

Sell on upside gain of 5.0 % (after a downturn) or when loss > 15.0 %

These criteria if followed provided a 12 Month Gain of 40.57 %

Buy  on 07/08/10 @ 19.22
Sell on 07/21/10 @ 21.27 for gain of 2.05/Share or 10.67 %

Buy  on 10/01/10 @ 23.59
Sell on 11/09/10 @ 26.28 for gain of 2.69/Share or 11.40 %

Buy  on 01/31/11 @ 28.71
Sell on 02/04/11 @ 30.84 for gain of 2.13/Share or 7.42 %

Buy  on 02/24/11 @ 32.49
Sell on 03/28/11 @ 34.28 for gain of 1.79/Share or 5.51 %

Buy  on 04/19/11 @ 32.77
Sell on 06/01/11 @ 34.51 for gain of 1.74/Share or 5.31 %

Buy  on 06/07/11 @ 33.79
Waiting to Sell        Current Gain of 0.27 %
```

So finding stocks to invest in based on the technical aspect is not the problem. The issue is, "Are you comfortable investing in this particular company right now?" Is it on your prospect list? Does it fit your criteria of a good company? These are very important questions that need answers for continuous success.

Once you narrow your opportunity list to a group that fits your investment criteria, the VTAM Black Box can provide you with the buy and sell indications that have generated excellent returns in the past. The fundamentals that I like when selecting companies for investment are provided in the chapter Fundamental Analysis.

With the major correction in Netflix in the fall of 2011, the question is, "What did the VTAM Black Box show during this period?" The data was updated just before the book went to press. Here is the new NFLX chart. The VTAM Black Box would have taken you out of NFLX long before the great fall. Your 12-month return would be an acceptable 32% and you would have avoided a significant loss.

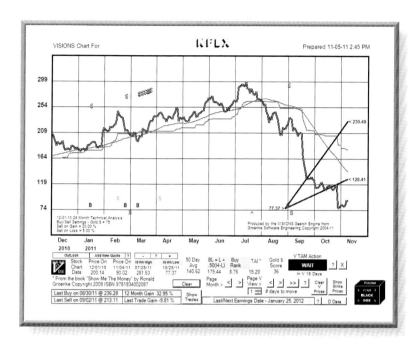

VTAM Black Box
in Action

"With self-discipline most anything is possible."

Theodore Roosevelt

Now that you have studied the concept and process of when to Buy and when to Sell any stock or ETF, lets review some examples of opportunities that provided a generous return during a recent twelve-month period.

These are all very well established companies in their sectors. Some have two or three trades and others have up to eight trades in a year. This demonstrates the concept that each stock trades in its own unique pattern with repetitive up and down cycles.

Here is AXP (American Express). Eight trades were provided which resulted in a 12-month return of over 40%.

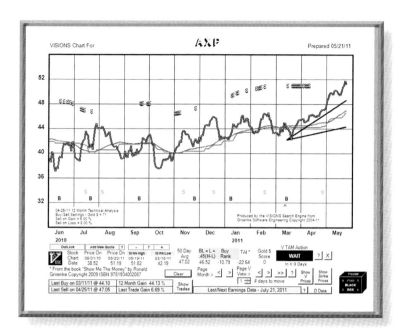

Here are the details on the trades.

```
VISIONS Chart Buy/Sell Trade Report for AXP on 05/26/11

Buy Limit Fraction = 0.45 and High/Low Range = 10 weeks.

Buy when number of up days = 3, trading in the Groenke V for 20 days,
currently trading in the V or within +/- 5.0 % of the 50 day average,
and with a VISIONS Chart Gold $ Score that is >= 71.

Sell on upside gain of 6.0 % (after a downturn) or when loss > 8.0 %

These criteria if followed provided a 12 Month Gain of 44.13 %

Buy  on 06/11/10 @ 39.44
Sell on 07/14/10 @ 43.14 for gain of 3.70/Share or 9.38 %

Buy  on 07/20/10 @ 41.53
Sell on 08/03/10 @ 44.03 for gain of 2.50/Share or 6.02 %

Buy  on 09/16/10 @ 40.44
Sell on 11/08/10 @ 43.55 for gain of 3.11/Share or 7.69 %

Buy  on 11/19/10 @ 42.41
Sell on 12/14/10 @ 45.83 for gain of 3.42/Share or 8.06 %

Buy  on 01/04/11 @ 43.60
Sell on 02/14/11 @ 46.34 for gain of 2.74/Share or 6.28 %

Buy  on 03/11/11 @ 44.10
Sell on 04/25/11 @ 47.05 for gain of 2.95/Share or 6.69 %
```

There are six completed trades. In reviewing the chart it is interesting to note that the stock was trading at 46 twelve months ago, and now is at the same or lower price. This again proves that Buy and Hold was not a valid strategy for this stock. With the VISIONS VTAM Black Box a 40% or better return was possible during the same period. So the pattern for this stock is short hold times to capture the ups and downs between $47 and $38.

Here is AA (Alcoa). Two trades were provided with a 12-month return of over 40%. Note the last sell. Stock was flat and started a downturn and still has not established a new major up cycle. Patience tells us to wait for a Buy indication on the next positive up cycle. Here we have a pattern of long times between buy and sell. They are quite different then that of AXP.

```
VISIONS Chart Buy/Sell Trade Report for AA on 04/16/11

Buy Limit Fraction = 0.45 and High/Low Range = 52 weeks.

Buy when number of up days = 3, trading in the Groenke V for 20 days,
currently trading in the V or within +/- 5.0 % of the 50 day average,
and with a VISIONS Chart Gold $ Score that is >= 71.

Sell on upside gain of 20.0 % (after a downturn) or when loss > 15.0 %

These criteria if followed provided a 12 Month Gain of 47.53 %

Buy  on 05/25/10 @ 11.30
Sell on 11/08/10 @ 13.96 for gain of 2.66/Share or 23.54 %

Buy  on 11/10/10 @ 13.88
Sell on 02/02/11 @ 17.21 for gain of 3.33/Share or 23.99 %
```

Here is URE (2X Dow Jones U.S. Real Estate SM Index ETF). Five trades were provided with a 12-month return of over 50%. Note how this ETF trades in one channel for some time and then went to a new channel. The latest one is in the 57 to 64 range. It's a great opportunity for the investor selling covered calls and naked puts to take advantage of the excellent at-the-money (ATM) premiums.

Here is AMZN (Amazon.com, Inc). Five trades in the last 12 months with an overall 59% return. Note the big up and down swings. This is an excellent VTAM Black Box stock. Great fundamentals and a trading pattern with short hold times. The result for 24 months also shows that one can generate substantial gains for a long time.

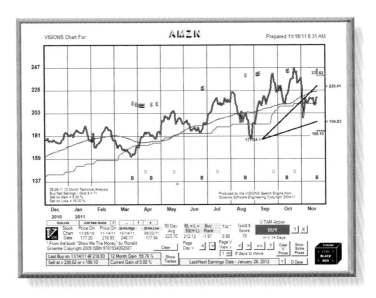

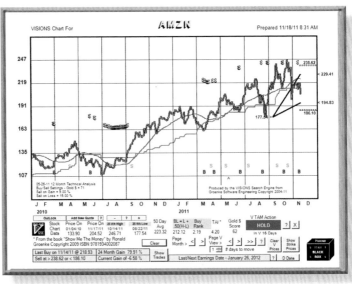

Here is <u>GG (Goldcorp Inc)</u>. Five trades in the last 12 months with an overall 65% return. Note the sell points. Out just before the major fall in price. This is <u>another excellent</u> VTAM Black Box stock.

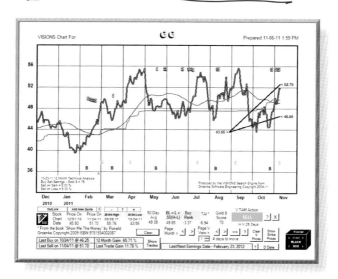

Here is GMCR (Green Mountain Coffee Roasters, Inc). A great return if the buy and sell signals are followed. "Did the VTAM Black Box indicate the last sell too early?" The second GMCR chart shows that it was the right time to sell. Three more buys and then out with a small loss before the big drop.

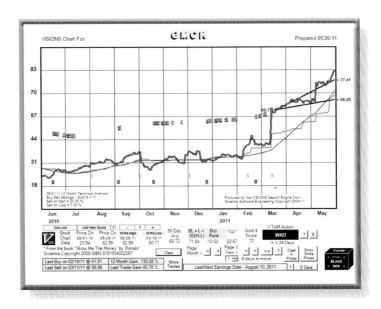

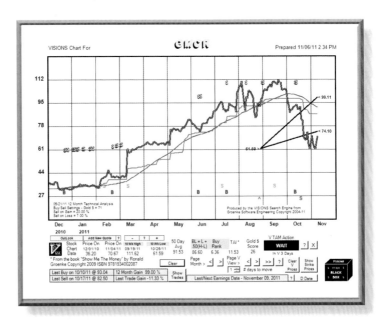

Here is BIIB (Biogen Idec Inc.). Three trades in the 12-month period. For a large portion of this twelve period the stock was flat at about $66.

But the VTAM Black Box captured the big upswing in April and again the one in October. Then out at the right time with the gain in the bank.

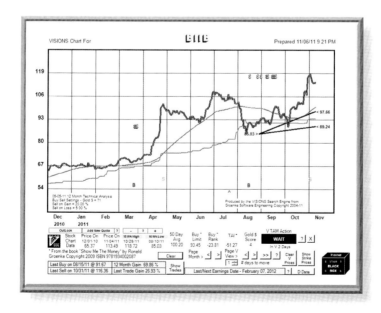

Here is FAS (3X Russell 1000 Financial Services Index ETF). Five trades with a 65% return. Very short hold times reduces the risk and exposure to world events.

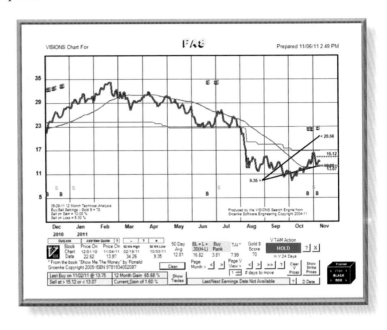

Fundamental Analysis

*"If you want to succeed you should strike out on new paths,
rather than travel the worn paths of accepted success."*

John D. Rockefeller

How do you find good stocks to invest in? Well, do not invest in stocks or stock symbols, invest in companies. The question is, "How do you find good companies to invest in?"

There are many ways to analyze the fundamentals of any company. In many cases it is personal preference on what to look for and what is important.

The criteria I provide are based on my experience in trying to generate consistent returns in all types of markets and economic conditions. I consider myself a conservative investor. I do not like to lose money, so my criteria may at first appear to be rather restrictive. I did experience a number of losses in the early period of my investing experience and therefore developed and refined a set of criteria that has reduced the risk significantly. The biggest risk in any investment is the probability that the company fails and goes bankrupt. The biggest failures recently are General Motors and Chrysler. So it does happen. These were big companies. The frequency for smaller company failure is even greater. That is why I place a lot of importance on company size in terms of capitalization and level of sales or revenue per year. I want to invest in stable companies that are growing their revenue and have

tive quarterly earnings. I also like companies that are followed
\e options market. This gives me another alternative to generate
acceptable returns on my investment.

Here are seven important fundamentals I think a company needs
to pass to be on one's prospect list.

1) Revenue or sales of at least $250M per year (>$500M is
desired).
2) Market Cap of $500M or more (>$750M is desired).
3) Positive revenue growth (>15% is desired).
4) Positive earnings for three of the last four quarters.
(Positive earnings for the last four quarters are desired).
5) Positive Bare Cash. Bare Cash is cash plus marketable
securities less long term debt (>$100M is desired).
6) Trading volume of at least 250,000 shares per day (>500K
desired).
7) Options available.

Note that I have stated what is acceptable and what is desired. If I
can find sufficient opportunities at the desired level, I believe my risk
is greatly reduced.

The key to success is to invest in good companies that will be around
for the long haul and that can sustain recessions and market corrections. The criteria above have been put to the test in two major market
corrections. The first one was in 2001 and the second one in 2009. The
criteria kept me out of the *.com* stocks of the late '90s since most of the
high flyers did not have any revenue let alone positive earnings. The
criteria also signaled the problem of the financials with poor earnings
and negative revenue growth in early 2008.

I have been told my criteria are too restrictive and do not allow one
to participate in those companies whose stock price is doubling every
six months. This may be the case, but that is part of the risk reward
equation. You can always have a few speculative stocks in your portfolio, but do not make that your strategy for long-term success. If you
go all-in on some high flyers you may be lucky and win. But then again
you may lose. I do not invest based on luck. You cannot buy a stock and
HOPE or WISH the stock price up. In most cases it will move based
on its fundamentals in the market place and demand for the stock by
the buyers and sellers, which is something you have no control over.

What is missing from my list? The two major items are price to earnings ratio and dividends.

I look at P/E but do not use it as one of the selection criteria. The main reason is that there are inconsistencies in how P/E is viewed.

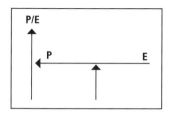

Here is what happens when the value of P and E change. If stock price P is going down, then P/E goes down. Good or Bad?

If stock price P is going up, then P/E goes up. Good or Bad?

If earnings E is going down, then P/E goes up. Good or Bad?

But if E goes down, then P is likely to go down also.

If earnings E is going up, then P/E goes down. Good or Bad?

But if E goes up, then P is likely to go up also.

So if E is missed, P goes down (caused by the market, no one likes it when E is missed) and then P/E goes down. Good or Bad?

Too many companies control the E through accounting.

Earnings could be negative the last two quarters and positive three and four quarters ago causing a low P/E. So low P/E could be misleading. I like to ask the following: Is revenue growing? What are the earnings swing?

It has been my observation that companies that are increasing their revenue are growing. They are doing something in the marketplace to gain market share. Companies that downsize to improve earnings are on the wrong side of the equation. The short term may look good, but it does nothing for future growth. Spending time trying to maintain stock price only works for a few quarters. Good companies grow by growing sales and revenue, not by cutting costs.

"What about dividends?" Dividends are good but not a deciding factor in my book. They add to overall return on the investment but are minimal at best. The average dividend for the companies in the S&P 500 is about 2.20%. Waiting to collect this each quarter instead of selling a position may actually reduce your overall gain. This is one of the reasons I like companies that also have stock options available. I can sell calls on my positions and generate my own dividends from option premiums each month. I use this strategy rather frequently for good companies when they are trading in a tight range.

Another factor that one may want to review is Beta. Beta measures a stock's volatility, the degree to which its price fluctuates in relation to the overall market.

Beta is also used to compare a stock's market risk to that of other stocks.

This measure is calculated using regression analysis. A beta of one (1) indicates that the security's price tends to move with the market. A beta greater than 1 indicates that the security's price tends to be more volatile than the market and a beta less than 1 means it tends to be less volatile than the market.

For example, let's say a company has a beta of 2. This means it is two times as volatile as the overall market. Let's say we expect the market to provide a return of 10% on an investment. We would expect the company to return 20%. On the other hand, if the market were to decline and provide a return of –6%, investors in that company could expect a return of –12% (a loss of 12%). If a stock had a beta of 0.5, we would expect it to be half as volatile as the market: a market return of 10% would mean a 5% gain for the company.

So high beta stocks usually have wider stock price swings and indicate higher risk. The time for caution is when this indication gets rather large (like >4). I measure beta or risk with a concept I call Probability of price Achievement. I have found this to be a much better way to gauge how stock prices may go up or down in the future. This concept has significant merit and is presented in detail in the Probability of Success chapter. There, I define P of A (Probability of price Achievement) for stocks and also show how it can be used to select option strike prices and strike dates for improved success with option trades.

Probability of Success

"Things do not happen. Things are made to happen."

John F. Kennedy

Did you ever buy a stock and hope that it goes up? Most everyone has been there. The concept of Hope and Luck is good, but will not pay the bills. How about a concept that gives you a look into the future before you invest in a stock? This is something that I have worked on for a long time. I have written many programs and spreadsheets to analyze stock prices and stock trends. I even developed a program called the Stock Market Simulator that analyzed past stock history and tried to forecast the future with economic influences like interest rates, unemployment rates, consumer sentiment, etc. It provided great value and insight to the bigger picture on where the market may be headed. I continue to use it to temper my expectations and help guide my investing decisions. While using that program, I developed another concept I call Probability of price Achievement or P of A.

What is the probability that a stock will reach a certain price in a specific time frame? That is a very worthwhile piece of information that can improve your investment decisions. So rather than hope a stock goes up, you can look at the probability that the stock will reach your desired price sometime in the future by looking at its history.

Stocks trade in their own well-defined patterns. So if we look back in time, it will give us a picture of where the stock may trade in the future.

The calculation of Probability of price Achievement is as follows:

P of A = Probability of price Achievement

P of A = 100 *(PofA1 + PofA2)

P of A 1 = (Tdays-Fdays)/Tdays x Adays/Fdays

P of A 2 = Fdays/Tdays x Bdays/(Tdays-Fdays)

Where:

Fdays = Number of days into the future.

Tdays = Number of trading days in a one year period = 252

Adays = Number of days the stock price was above a specific price in the last Fdays.

Bdays = Number of days the stock price was above a specific price in the last Tdays up and until the last Fdays days.

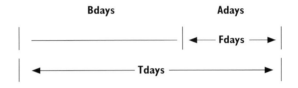

The concept here is that the stock price is likely to follow the pattern of the last Fdays. The number of times the stock price has traded above the chosen stock price is weighted by the number of days in the future versus the total number of days being considered.

A probability of less then .01 (1%) is possible when a stock has not traded above the chosen price for the period under consideration.

The following example demonstrates P of A.

Here is a chart for General Electric (GE) that shows the trading history for the last year.

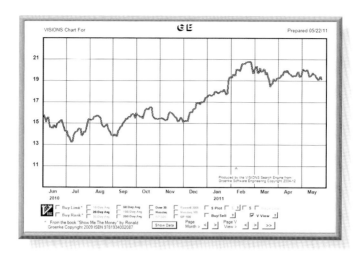

We can use this or the detail data provided to determine the values needed in the P of A calculation.

What is the probability that GE will trade at $20 or above in the next 30 days (about 20 trading days out?)

We determine Adays and Bdays as follows

Going back in time 20 trading days (Fdays = 20) we see that GE traded at or above $20 ten times (Adays = 10). For the other 232 days (Tdays = 252 −20) GE traded above $20 forty-seven times (Bdays =47).

P of A 1 = (Tdays-Fdays)/Tdays x Adays/Fdays

P of A 1 = (232 / 252) x (10/20) = .9206 x .50 = .4603

P of A 2 = Fdays/Tdays x Bdays/(Tdays-Fdays)

P of A 2 = (20 / 252) x (47/232) = .07936 x .202586 =. 0161

P of A = 100 *(PofA1 + PofA2)

P of A = 100 *(.4603 + .0161)

P of A = 47.64

Probability GE will be $20 or higher in 30 days is 47.64 %.

We can do this for any price and period of time. A summary of selected target prices is provided in the table below.

```
Probability of Price Achievement for GE on 05/25/11

Current Stock Price 19.22

  Probability in % Stock Price is Higher then Target

Target    <<<  For these Days into the Future  >>>
Price     30      60     120     180     240     300
-----   ------  ------  ------  ------  ------  ------
   15    98.84   97.38   93.49   86.93   74.41   57.07
   16    96.72   92.60   81.62   63.04   40.79   15.20
   17    95.35   89.51   73.97   47.49   24.27   10.01
   18    94.97   88.67   71.86   43.01   21.97    9.06
   19    94.32   87.20   67.59   35.23   17.99    7.42
   20    47.64   55.49   46.26   23.35   11.93    4.92
   21     0.31    0.69    7.40    3.69    1.88    0.78
   22     0.00    0.00    0.00    0.00    0.00    0.00
```

GE Historical Data

1/3/2011	18.15	2/22/2011	20.68	4/11/2011	20.18
1/4/2011	18.48	2/23/2011	20.23	4/12/2011	20.01
1/5/2011	18.51	2/24/2011	20.58	4/13/2011	19.94
1/6/2011	18.43	2/25/2011	20.82	4/14/2011	20
1/7/2011	18.3	2/28/2011	20.92	4/15/2011	20.04
1/10/2011	18.38	3/1/2011	20.25	4/18/2011	19.98
1/11/2011	18.5	3/2/2011	20.32	4/19/2011	20.27
1/12/2011	18.54	3/3/2011	20.75	4/20/2011	20.4
1/13/2011	18.47	3/4/2011	20.37	4/21/2011	19.95
1/14/2011	18.69	3/7/2011	20.38	4/25/2011	19.89
1/18/2011	18.47	3/8/2011	20.63	4/26/2011	20.1
1/19/2011	18.2	3/9/2011	20.63	4/27/2011	20.65
1/20/2011	18.3	3/10/2011	20.1	4/28/2011	20.6
1/21/2011	19.6	3/11/2011	20.36	4/29/2011	20.45
1/24/2011	19.9	3/14/2011	19.92	5/2/2011	20.48
1/25/2011	19.84	3/15/2011	19.61	5/3/2011	20.64
1/26/2011	19.78	3/16/2011	18.95	5/4/2011	20.27
1/27/2011	20.14	3/17/2011	19.22	5/5/2011	19.9
1/28/2011	20.06	3/18/2011	19.25	5/6/2011	20.01
1/31/2011	20	3/21/2011	19.72	5/9/2011	20.07
2/1/2011	20.66	3/22/2011	19.49	5/10/2011	20.3
2/2/2011	20.57	3/23/2011	19.53	5/11/2011	20.09
2/3/2011	20.61	3/24/2011	19.78	5/12/2011	20.14
2/4/2011	20.42	3/25/2011	19.75	5/13/2011	19.89
2/7/2011	20.73	3/28/2011	19.75	5/16/2011	19.76
2/8/2011	21.13	3/29/2011	19.86	5/17/2011	19.59
2/9/2011	21.16	3/30/2011	20.11	5/18/2011	19.76
2/10/2011	21.12	3/31/2011	20.05	5/19/2011	19.96
2/11/2011	21.18	4/1/2011	20.34	5/20/2011	19.62
2/14/2011	21.35	4/4/2011	20.53	5/23/2011	19.39
2/15/2011	21.31	4/5/2011	20.33	5/24/2011	19.1
2/16/2011	21.29	4/6/2011	20.55	5/25/2011	19.22
2/17/2011	21.37	4/7/2011	20.35		
2/18/2011	21.29	4/8/2011	20.19		

This probability table provides guidance in our investment decision process. For example, it shows the probability that GE moves up to $21 or higher in the near term is very low (< 1%). As a result, buying at this time and hoping that the price is going to move beyond $21 any time soon is very shortsighted. Even at 120 days out, the probability that GE is at $21 or above is less than 10%. So a Buy and Hold may not be very productive. A covered call at $20 or $21 however may be appropriate since the table shows that GE may not move up in price very fast.

If we can determine the probability, a call or put option will be assigned at various strike prices and strike dates we can make decisions that will improve our success with option trades. A very useful tool for improving the success of option trades.

P of A for Options

The P of A concept can be applied in the use of call or put options to determine the probability a call or put option will be assigned or not. The Call or Put Assignment probability calculation is similar to that for the probability of price achievement. The detail for the calculation is provided in Appendix A.

For call options the probability table is tailored to specific prices (strike prices) and dates (expiration dates).

Here are some call options for GE that go along with the chart shown above. It shows for options available, the premium being offered, the gain expected if called or expired, the number of days to expiration, and the probability of assignment. So now you have additional data to make intelligent decisions.

It shows for example that the probability of a June $20 call being assigned is only 39.83 %. That option returns 3.39% if called or a .62% return if expired. That compares to a July $20 call that returns 4.16% if called, or 1.39% if expired, with a 55.36% probability of assignment. The latter may be a better choice. Doing this a number of times during the year could add up to a very meaningful return.

Call Options for GENERAL ELECTRIC CO. [GE] On 05/27/11 10:30 AM Price < 50DAvg TAI=Bad Idea
Price 19.46 (+0.04) 52WkHi 21.65 52WkLow 13.75 50DayAvg 19.97 BuyLimit 15.72 BuyRank -18.94 Gold $ 50 Beta 1.82

Option RefSym	Strike Date	Strike Price	Call Option Premium Bid	Asked	Open Intrst	% Gain If Sold	% Gain If Exprd	Days Till Exp	Best Fit	Break Even Price	Probability of being Assigned(%)	Number of A-Days	Number of B-Days	Number of T-Days
YGE016	6/17/11	18.00	1.48	1.52	17,281	0.10	7.61	22		17.98	95.78	17	88	252
YGE017	6/17/11	19.00	0.59	0.61	35,580	0.67	3.03	22	*	18.87	95.23	17	69	252
YGE018	6/17/11	20.00	0.12	0.13	73,648	3.39	0.62	22		19.34	39.83	7	50	252
YGE027	7/15/11	17.00	2.47	2.51	388	0.05	12.69	50	*	16.99	90.71	37	79	252
YGE028	7/15/11	18.00	1.54	1.56	3,195	0.41	7.91	50	*	17.92	89.96	37	68	252
YGE029	7/15/11	19.00	0.76	0.77	6,901	1.54	3.91	50		18.70	88.66	37	49	252
YGE030	7/15/11	20.00	0.27	0.28	14,964	4.16	1.39	50		19.19	55.36	23	34	252
YGE031	7/15/11	21.00	0.07	0.08	21,880	8.27	0.36	50	*	19.39	< 1.00	0	9	252
YGE038	8/19/11	17.00	2.55	2.59	814	0.46	13.10	85	*	16.91	82.76	61	55	252
YGE039	8/19/11	18.00	1.70	1.73	2,848	1.23	8.74	85	*	17.76	81.37	61	44	252
YGE040	8/19/11	19.00	1.00	1.02	3,533	2.77	5.14	85		18.46	77.85	60	26	252
YGE041	8/19/11	20.00	0.51	0.53	14,913	5.40	2.62	85		18.95	46.28	35	22	252
YGE042	8/19/11	21.00	0.23	0.24	7,493	9.10	1.18	85	*	19.23	1.14	0	9	252
YGE043	8/19/11	22.00	0.09	0.10	3,409	13.51	0.46	85	*	19.37	< 1.00	0	0	252
YGE054	9/16/11	16.00	3.50	3.60	1,582	0.21	17.99	113	*	15.96	81.95	81	75	252
YGE055	9/16/11	17.00	2.63	2.67	3,150	0.87	13.51	113	*	16.83	74.44	81	35	252
YGE056	9/16/11	18.00	1.83	1.87	11,277	1.90	9.40	113		17.63	72.37	81	24	252
YGE057	9/16/11	19.00	1.17	1.19	18,619	3.65	6.01	113		18.29	68.15	80	6	252
YGE058	9/16/11	20.00	0.66	0.68	27,598	6.17	3.39	113	*	18.80	46.45	55	2	252
YGE059	9/16/11	21.00	0.34	0.36	21,744	9.66	1.75	113	*	19.12	7.54	9	0	252
YGE060	9/16/11	22.50	0.11	0.12	37,347	16.19	0.57	113		19.35	< 1.00	0	0	252

Here is the data for some GE put options with the probability that a put will be assigned.

Taking a look at the put data we see that a 1% return is possible with a June $19 put with a probability of 4.77% that it would be assigned in 22 days.

A July $19 put provides a 2.21% return in 50 days with an 11.34% probability of being assigned. I would do the June $19 put since I get to make a new decision again in 22 days, versus being exposed to a possible downturn in the 50 days until the July expiration. This allows me to repeat the smaller gain with new information such as, my yearly return would be as good as or better with less exposure to risk. The key is to understand the return for the risk. This will improve your success over time.

Put Options for GENERAL ELECTRIC CO. [GE] On 05/27/11 1:37 PM Price < 50DAvg TAI=Bad Idea
Price 19.49 (+0.07) 52wkHi 21.65 52wkLow 13.75 50DayAvg 19.97 BL 15.72 BR -19.09 Gold $ 50 Beta 1.82

Option RefSym	Strike Date	Strike Price	Put Option Premium Bid	Asked	Open Interest	Put Factor	Percent Discount	Days Till Exp	Best Fit	Price If Asgnd	Probability of being Assigned(%)	Number of A-Days	Number of B-Days	Number of T-Days
FGE023	06/03/11	20.00	0.52	0.57	103	-1.39	2.60	8		19.48	99.28	8	189	252
FGE037	6/17/11	18.00	0.05	0.06	34391	0.18	0.28	22		17.95	4.22	0	147	252
FGE038	6/17/11	19.00	0.19	0.20	54710	0.20	1.00	22		18.81	4.77	0	166	252
FGE039	6/17/11	20.00	0.76	0.78	63409	-0.74	3.80	22		19.24	60.22	10	187	252
FGE040	6/17/11	21.00	1.67	1.71	29616	-4.37	7.95	22		19.33	99.74	17	226	252
FGE048	7/15/11	17.00	0.08	0.09	9220	0.23	0.47	50		16.92	9.29	0	136	252
FGE049	7/15/11	18.00	0.17	0.18	7324	0.26	0.94	50		17.83	10.04	0	147	252
FGE050	7/15/11	19.00	0.42	0.43	15919	0.19	2.21	50		18.58	11.34	0	166	252
FGE051	7/15/11	20.00	0.93	0.95	14729	-0.40	4.65	50		19.07	47.02	15	182	252
FGE052	7/15/11	21.00	1.72	1.76	2534	-1.98	8.19	50		19.28	99.39	37	206	252
FGE053	7/15/11	22.00	2.66	2.71	1882	-4.63	12.09	50		19.34	100.00	37	215	252
FGE054	7/15/11	23.00	3.65	3.70	1180	-8.14	15.87	50		19.35	100.00	37	215	252
FGE058	8/19/11	13.00	0.05	0.06	435	0.38	0.38	85		12.95	< 1.00	0	0	252
FGE059	8/19/11	15.00	0.09	0.10	465	0.35	0.60	85		14.91	4.31	0	34	252
FGE060	8/19/11	16.00	0.13	0.14	1359	0.35	0.81	85		15.87	12.17	0	96	252
FGE061	8/19/11	17.00	0.21	0.23	16095	0.36	1.24	85		16.79	17.24	0	136	252
FGE062	8/19/11	18.00	0.38	0.39	7625	0.35	2.11	85		17.62	18.63	0	147	252
FGE063	8/19/11	19.00	0.68	0.70	8033	0.18	3.58	85		18.32	22.15	1	165	252
FGE064	8/19/11	20.00	1.18	1.19	16363	-0.30	5.90	85		18.82	55.09	27	170	252
FGE065	8/19/11	21.00	1.88	1.91	1682	-1.27	8.95	85		19.12	98.86	61	182	252
FGE066	8/19/11	22.00	2.73	2.78	1184	-2.80	12.41	85		19.27	100.00	61	191	252
FGE067	8/19/11	23.00	3.65	3.75	440	-4.79	15.87	85		19.35	100.00	61	191	252
FGE068	8/19/11	24.00	4.55	4.75	0	-7.04	18.96	85		19.45	100.00	61	191	252
FGE069	8/19/11	25.00	5.55	5.75	0	-9.67	22.20	85		19.45	100.00	61	191	252

Looking into the Future

How about a crystal ball for determining future stock prices or direction? Another opportunity to get an advantage when making investment decisions is available with a technique called OutLook. We take the P of A process one step further and project the price of any stock or ETF out fifty days in time. The process looks at the price movement the last 50 trading days and projects the stock motion forward with a Monte Carlo simulation technique. You select the trend for the outlook based on the current stock direction or trends of major indexes.

Here is an example with American Express (AXP). An outlook was created on 4-15-2011. It indicated that AXP should be in the 46–47 range fifty days out. The actual result was around 48, which shows that OutLook did a great job of showing what might happen. This view can help in your selection of option strike date and strike price thus increasing the number of successful trades.

OutLook is available on any VISIONS chart.

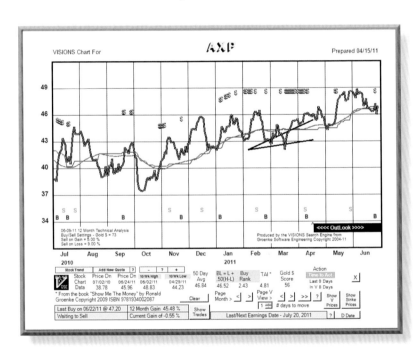

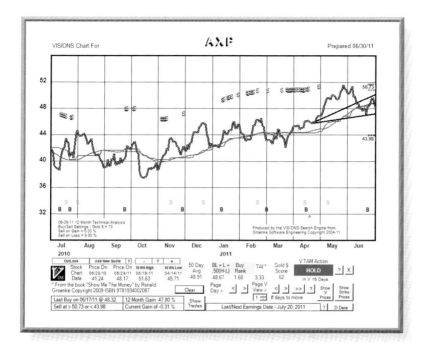

Show Me the Trade

"Simplicity is the ultimate sophistication."
Leonardo da Vinci

Everyone wants to be successful when investing his or her hard-earned money. But, just for the record, it takes a lot more than luck and hot stock tips. It takes knowledge, strategy, planning, and a sense of the world around us for one to be continuously successful. The key is to plan for the worst and not get greedy. These two principles have always been front and foremost in all of the processes that I have used myself and provided as tools for other investors. They are imbedded in the equations and search processes used to provide the highest probability of success for each type of trade presented in the following chapters.

The next chapter, Buy-Hold-Sell, allows you to take the results of the VTAM Black Box and prepare an investment plan for any portfolio of stocks and ETF's. I will show how to implement a variety of strategies that use options to enhance your gain and well-being. I use the covered call strategy as a way to get into a position based on the Black Box Buy signal and then use the sell parameters to select the option strike price that automatically takes the gain to the bank if the stock moves up as planned. I personally like the Double Up strategy most of all. It has generated continuous gains in all types of markets (up, flat, or down). Buy some now and then more at a later time, if the price moves down.

If the price moves up you still have a two for one gain with downside protection. If the price moves down you buy more at a discount and then sell calls to generate a very acceptable return.

I developed the Open Fence strategy that requires tolerance for risk, but can be very successful since stocks do not move up and down at the same time. One half of the trade is always successful and both are successful if the stock trades in a channel. Find those stocks or ETF's that trade in a tight range and you can take a lot of money to the bank.

The VISIONS TradeXpress program provided the examples for each strategy. This Trade Planner feature implements the algorithms for option selection in conjunction with the Probability of price Achievement (P of A). It optimizes the possible return by searching the option tables for the best strike price and strike date combinations that generate the highest return in the shortest time possible and allows you to quickly formulate a set of trades for your investment plan.

The examples provided include the cost of trading (commissions) at a typical discount brokerage firm. The returns shown are net after these costs and try to represent what is possible.

To experience examples for yourself in real time, you can install a free copy of VISIONS on your PC now. This will allow you to review each strategy with data for your stocks of interest. This puts you in the driver's seat and allows you to prepare trades that you could execute right now.

Why wait? Let the fun begin!

Buy-Hold-Sell

"Create your own vision of happiness."

Jean Groenke

STRATEGY: Buy a stock and wait for price appreciation.

OUTLOOK: Expecting the stock to move up.

PROFIT: The return is the price appreciation in the stock.

RISK: Risk is related to stock ownership. Worst case is stock goes to zero. To exit this trade, sell the position.

BREAKEVEN: Stock purchase price.

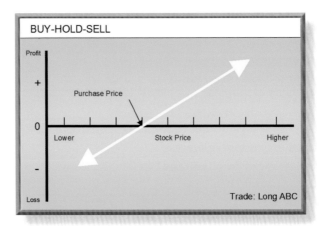

The Buy-Hold-Sell strategy can be simple and straightforward or as complex as desired. You buy a stock at one price, hold for some time, and then sell. The purchase price sets the cost basis and the exit price determines whether there is a gain or loss on the asset. The gains, if any, are realized only when the asset is sold. Until that time there is the possibility of partial or total loss of the investment if the price of the stock goes to zero. This trade needs to be monitored and may need action in case something bad happens to the stock price.

The reason for using this particular strategy is that you are bullish on the stock and the equity market as a whole. You can hope the stock goes up but there is nothing you can do to actually lift it up. You can however use the P of A concept to help in your decision process.

To be successful with this strategy the price of the stock you have purchased must go up. Before making an investment in a good company, review the probability the stock price may reach your target. If the probability is low, it may not be a good idea to invest at this time.

For example let's look at a possible investment in Caterpillar (CAT) or Deere (DE). The VTAM Black Box signaled a BUY for both on May 27, 2011. The charts and P of A tables are provided below.

In reviewing CAT we see that it made a recent high of $115 about a month back and is now trading at $105. If we invest now, how likely is it that we can earn a 5% return in 60 days? To get a 5% return, CAT needs to move up to $110. It traded above that a few times in the last 30 days. When looking at the P of A table we move down to the $110 price target and check the 30 and 60 day time period. The probability that CAT achieves $110 is about 28 to 30 percent in 30 to 60 days.

Let's compare this with a possible invest in DE. DE needs to get to $90 for a 5% return. Reviewing the data in the P of A table for DE we see the probability of DE moving to $90 in 30 to 60 days is about 48 to 60 percent. This is almost twice that of CAT. That very interesting information can help in our investment decision process. There is always the possibility things do not move as expected, but this additional information may improve success.

Further review of the charts and P of A tables shows the opportunity for significant gains of 20% or more are highly unlikely. For CAT the probability it moves up 10% in 60 days is less then 5 %. For DE the probability it moves up 10% is somewhat better at about 25% in 60 days.

Here is an example of the analysis with some potential trades.

```
Buy-Hold-Sell for DE on 05/27/11 3:29 PM


Buy 1000 DE @ 85.74                              -85745.00
Probability Price < or = 82.50 in 47 Days =       8.96 %
Probability Price > or = 92.50 in 47 Days =      45.95 %
Return at 92.50 = 6713.58            7.83% (60.81 APR)
-----------------------------------------------------------


Buy 1000 DE @ 85.74                              -85745.00
Probability Price < or = 82.50 in 19 Days =       3.77 %
Probability Price > or = 92.50 in 19 Days =      12.84 %
Return at 92.50 = 6713.58           7.83% (150.41 APR)



Buy-Hold-Sell for CAT on 05/27/11 3:35 PM

Buy 1000 CAT @ 104.60                           -104605.00
Probability Price < or = 100.00 in 47 Days =     11.33 %
Probability Price > or = 110.00 in 47 Days =     25.05 %
Return at 110.00 = 5348.86           5.11% (39.71 APR)
-----------------------------------------------------------

Buy 1000 CAT @ 104.60                           -104605.00
Probability Price < or = 100.00 in 19 Days =      4.76 %
Probability Price > or = 110.00 in 19 Days =     17.94 %
Return at 110.00 = 5348.86           5.11% (98.23 APR)
-----------------------------------------------------------
```

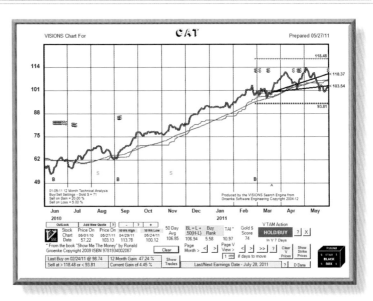

```
Probability of Price Achievement for CAT on 05/27/11

Current Stock Price 104.60

   Probability in % Stock Price is Higher then Target

Target    <<< For these Days into the Future  >>>
Price     30     60    120    180    240    300
-----   ------ ------ ------ ------ ------ ------
   95   94.39  87.35  68.61  36.05  18.41   7.59
   96   94.25  87.05  67.84  34.41  17.58   7.25
   97   94.18  86.89  67.46  33.59  17.16   7.07
   98   94.12  86.74  65.81  32.77  16.74   6.90
   99   94.05  86.58  64.17  31.95  16.32   6.73
  100   93.84  86.12  59.23  29.49  15.06   6.21
  101   93.64  85.66  54.30  27.04  13.81   5.69
  102   84.26  81.19  48.54  24.17  12.34   5.09
  103   79.45  78.68  42.78  21.30  10.88   4.49
  104   74.68  74.29  37.84  18.84   9.62   3.97
  105   60.83  68.09  34.55  17.20   8.79   3.62
  106   51.56  61.88  31.26  15.57   7.95   3.28
  107   42.22  53.56  26.33  13.11   6.70   2.76
  108   42.08  49.32  23.04  11.47   5.86   2.42
  109   37.30  41.00  18.10   9.01   4.60   1.90
  110   28.00  30.79  13.99   6.96   3.56   1.47
  111   18.69  22.54   9.87   4.92   2.51   1.04
  112   13.98  16.34   6.58   3.28   1.67   0.69
  113    9.24   6.13   2.47   1.23   0.63   0.26
  114    4.64   4.08   1.65   0.82   0.42   0.17
  115    0.03   2.04   0.82   0.41   0.21   0.09
  116    0.00   0.00   0.00   0.00   0.00   0.00
```

```
Probability of Price Achievement for DE on 05/27/11

Current Stock Price 85.74

  Probability in % Stock Price is Higher then Target
```

Target Price	<<<	For	these Days	into the	Future	>>>
	30	60	120	180	240	300
80	95.42	89.67	74.35	48.34	24.69	10.18
81	95.31	89.44	73.78	47.11	24.06	9.92
82	95.14	89.05	72.82	45.06	23.02	9.49
83	94.94	88.59	71.67	42.60	21.76	8.97
84	85.53	84.04	68.88	39.32	20.09	8.28
85	71.65	77.76	66.03	37.28	19.04	7.85
86	67.01	75.64	65.01	36.46	18.62	7.68
87	53.17	69.44	61.72	34.82	17.78	7.33
88	48.36	66.93	56.59	31.95	16.32	6.73
89	43.58	64.50	53.55	29.49	15.06	6.21
90	43.24	63.73	48.48	25.40	12.97	5.35
91	38.36	61.07	43.60	21.71	11.09	4.57
92	24.42	52.67	37.84	18.84	9.62	3.97
93	19.58	48.13	31.26	15.57	7.95	3.28
94	14.56	37.30	20.57	10.24	5.23	2.16
95	5.08	26.70	12.34	6.14	3.14	1.29
96	4.91	20.42	8.23	4.10	2.09	0.86
97	4.81	14.30	5.76	2.87	1.46	0.60
98	0.10	6.13	2.47	1.23	0.63	0.26
99	0.03	2.04	0.82	0.41	0.21	0.09
100	0.00	0.00	0.00	0.00	0.00	0.00

Here is an example of a Buy-Hold-Sell strategy for AMZN with trades in 2010 and 2011 as provided by the VTAM Black Box. The Black Box re-optimizes anytime a Wait is indicated to incorporate the lasted market condition and stock trend. The best Buy and Sell settings are then used for the next Buy-Hold-Sell cycle.

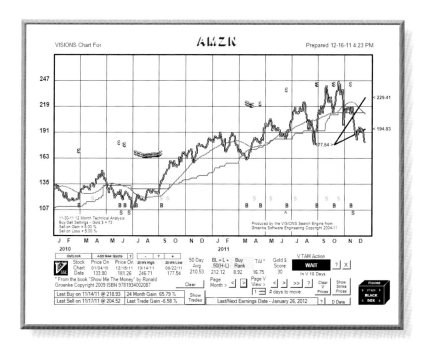

Trades for a 24-month period show that a 65% gain was possible. The gain for the last 12 months was over 40%. The 12-month rolling average gain starts at 20% and ends at 46% providing an opportunity to enter any cycle with a very acceptable gain for the next 12 months.

The detail of the trades are provided in the table that follows for your own further analysis as desired.

VISIONS Chart Buy/Sell Trade Report for AMZN on 12/16/11

Buy Limit Fraction = 0.50 and High/Low Range = 25 weeks.

Buy when number of up days = 3, trading in the Groenke V for 20 days, currently trading in the V or within +/- 5.0 % of the 50 day average, and with a VISIONS Chart Gold $ Score that is >= 73.

Sell on upside gain of 8.0 % (after a downturn) or when loss > 5.0 %

These criteria if followed provided a 24 Month Gain of 65.79 %

Buy on 03/02/10 @ 125.53
Sell on 03/31/10 @ 135.77 for gain of 10.24/Share or 8.16 %

Buy on 06/03/10 @ 128.76
Sell on 06/07/10 @ 122.01 for gain of -6.75/Share or -5.24 %

Buy on 06/15/10 @ 126.84
Sell on 06/24/10 @ 118.33 for gain of -8.51/Share or -6.71 %

Buy on 07/12/10 @ 119.51
Sell on 09/07/10 @ 137.22 for gain of 17.71/Share or 14.82 %

Buy on 09/08/10 @ 139.14
Sell on 09/21/10 @ 150.73 for gain of 11.59/Share or 8.33 %

Buy on 03/21/11 @ 164.52
Sell on 04/06/11 @ 182.76 for gain of 18.24/Share or 11.09 %

Buy on 04/20/11 @ 183.87
Sell on 05/13/11 @ 202.56 for gain of 18.69/Share or 10.16 %

Buy on 06/21/11 @ 194.23
Sell on 07/11/11 @ 212.55 for gain of 18.32/Share or 9.43 %

Buy on 08/29/11 @ 206.53
Sell on 09/20/11 @ 233.25 for gain of 26.72/Share or 12.94 %

Buy on 10/06/11 @ 221.51
Sell on 10/17/11 @ 242.33 for gain of 20.82/Share or 9.40 %

Buy on 11/14/11 @ 218.93
Sell on 11/17/11 @ 204.52 for gain of -14.41/Share or -6.58 %

Covered Call

"Always bear in mind that your own resolution to succeed is more important than any other."

Abraham Lincoln

STRATEGY: Buy a stock and sell a call at a strike price and strike date that provides monthly income.

OUTLOOK: Expecting a flat or slightly upward movement in the stock. If the call expires, sell another call a month out for income generation. If the call is assigned, review this or a different candidate for another covered call opportunity.

PROFIT: If the call expires, the return is the call option premium received. If assigned, the return is the option premium plus any price appreciation in the stock, which is limited by the strike price sold.

RISK: Risk is related to stock ownership. It is reduced by the amount of the call option premium received. Worst case is stock goes to zero. To exit this trade, buy the call back to close and sell the stock.

BREAKEVEN: Stock purchase price is less than the call option premium received.

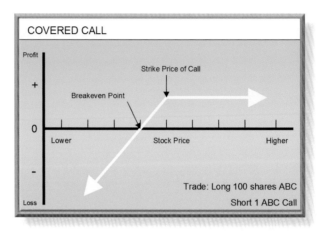

A Call Option is a contract that gives the holder the right (but not the obligation) to buy a specific stock at a predetermined price on or before a certain date (called the expiration date).

A Covered Call is a short call option position against a long position in the underlying stock or index where you are *willing to sell* your stock at a predetermined price.

A covered call is an investment strategy that provides the opportunity for an investor to generate a return on an investment without requiring an appreciation in the stock price. The primary motive is to earn premium income, which can increase the overall return on the stock and also provide a measure of downside protection. Once this trade is set, you can go on vacation and just let things happen.

The potential profit is capped by the call strike price but income is generated without taking on additional risk. The risk of loss is directly related to holding the stock and was assumed at the time the stock was first acquired. Selling a call option does not increase the downside risk. We again rely on fundamental analysis to direct us towards good solid companies to invest in.

One should view call assignment as a positive outcome since the planned or target exit price was achieved. The stock is liquidated at the preset price and the cash is available for investment again.

If the call is not assigned by expiration date, the process can be repeated and additional premium income can be earned by writing another call.

The covered call return is calculated as follows:

$$\text{If Sold} = \frac{(\text{Strike Price} + \text{Premium} - \text{Purchase Price})}{\text{Purchase Price}}$$

$$\text{If Expired} = \frac{\text{Premium}}{\text{Purchase Price}}$$

One of the elements for success in covered call writing is the selection of the strike price and the strike date. We now again look at the P of A concept and apply it to the covered call strategy. The question to be answered is "What is the probability the call will be assigned?" We look at the trading history for the stock and calculate the P of A for the strike price and strike date being considered. P of A in this case becomes Probability of Assignment.

For available call options, select the one that provides the desired return with the highest probability of assignment.

Here is an example.

We are willing to invest in Deere (DE) and want to write a call for income generation.

The following covered call trades are provided to demonstrate the analysis. The first table provides June options and the second table provides July options. The June calls only have a 30.88% chance of being assigned at $90, while the July options have a 61.67% chance of being called. The gain if called, is 6.37% in 47 days. If this is annualized the gain is over 45%. If DE does not reach our $90 price target, our gain is 1.45% in 47 days. That related to almost 12% a year. Sure beats CD rates.

```
Covered Call for DE on 05/27/11 3:29 PM

Buy 1000 DE @ 85.74                                      -85745.00
Sell 10 DE Jun 17 2011 90.00 Calls @ 0.50                  484.87
Prob. of Assignment = 30.88%       Called Value = 89958.58
OTM 19 Days to Expiration             Breakeven = 85260.13
----------------- Covered Call Return ------------------
If Sold Gain    =    4698.45             5.48% (105.27 APR)
If Expired Gain =     484.87             0.57% (10.86 APR)
-----------------------------------------------------------

Buy 1000 DE @ 85.74                                      -85745.00
Sell 10 DE Jun 17 2011 92.50 Calls @ 0.21                  194.95
Prob of Assignment = 12.84%        Called Value = 92458.58
OTM 19 Days to Expiration             Breakeven = 85550.05
----------------- Covered Call Return ------------------
If Sold Gain    =    6908.53             8.06% (154.78 APR)
If Expired Gain =     194.95             0.23% (4.37 APR)
-----------------------------------------------------------
```

```
Covered Call for DE on 05/27/11 3:29 PM

Buy 1000 DE @ 85.74                                      -85745.00
Sell 10 DE Jul 15 2011 90.00 Calls @ 1.26                 1244.68
Prob of Assignment = 61.67%        Called Value = 89958.58
OTM 47 Days to Expiration             Breakeven = 84500.32
----------------- Covered Call Return ------------------
If Sold Gain    =    5458.26             6.37% (49.44 APR)
If Expired Gain =    1244.68             1.45% (11.27 APR)
-----------------------------------------------------------

Buy 1000 DE @ 85.74                                      -85745.00
Sell 10 DE Jul 15 2011 92.50 Calls @ 0.70                  684.82
Prob of Assignment = 45.95%        Called Value = 92458.58
OTM 47 Days to Expiration             Breakeven = 85060.18
----------------- Covered Call Return ------------------
If Sold Gain    =    7398.40             8.63% (67.01 APR)
If Expired Gain =     684.82             0.80% (6.20 APR)
-----------------------------------------------------------
```

If I buy DE and sell a July call, I earn a minimum of 1.45% while waiting for DE to get to $90. I could also do this for a target price of $92.50 with a probability of assignment of 45.95%. Less than 1 out of 2 times that will happen. If it does not get assigned my return is only .80% in 47 days. I would select the lower strike price and take the premium to the bank. If the stock surged up and assignment took place the additional appreciation is like getting a bonus. I planned for a 1.45% return and get over four times that.

To learn more on how to invest using options I suggest you read my book *Show Me the Money—Covered Calls & Naked Puts for a Monthly Cash Income*, ISBN 9781934002087.

Naked Put

*"He who is not courageous enough to take risks
will accomplish nothing in life."*

Muhammad Ali

STRATEGY: Sell a put on a stock you have an interest in owning for monthly income. Pick a strike price about 5–10% below where it is currently trading. This allows a cushion in case the stock dips.

OUTLOOK: Expecting a flat or slightly upward movement in the stock. If the put expires, sell another put a month out for income generation. If the put is assigned, review the outlook for the stock and sell a call or roll out.

PROFIT: If the put expires, the return is the put option premium received. If assigned, the return is the option premium received divided by the assigned price.

RISK: Risk is related to stock ownership. If assigned, the purchase price is reduced by the amount of the put option premium received. Worst case is stock goes to zero. To exit this trade, buy the put back to close.

BREAKEVEN: The stock purchase price less the put option premium received.

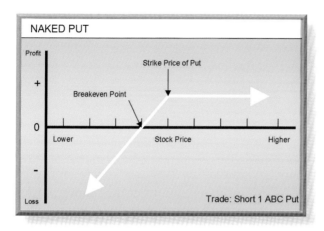

A Put Option is a contract that gives the holder the right (but not the obligation) to sell a specific stock at a predetermined price on or before a certain date (called the expiration date).

A Naked (Uncovered) Put is a short put option in which the writer does not have a corresponding short position on the underlying security. You are *willing to buy* a stock at a predetermined price.

The naked put strategy allows an investor to earn a return without ever owning the asset. The objective is to earn income on the margin in a margin brokerage account by selling puts on a stock of a good company that you have an interest in owning. This trade needs to be monitored and may need action if the stock price approaches the put strike price and assignment is not wanted.

The naked put strike price is selected based on the probability of assignment and not on the opportunity of maximizing premium income. The higher the put strike price the greater the premium, but with increased probability of assignment.

If a put option is assigned, the stock is purchased at a lower price than the price at the time the put was sold. You are buying a stock in a good company at a discount. The position can be held or becomes a candidate for a covered call.

You can also roll out by selling the position and then selling another put a few months out at the same or lower strike price. This provides additional premium income while waiting for the stock to recover.

Some option analysts try to convince you that the return on a naked put is infinity since no investment is needed. That is true only after the fact, when the put expires. In the real world the naked put needs to be backed up with some type of asset like cash or margin.

The naked put return is calculated as follows:

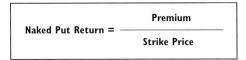

$$\text{Naked Put Return} = \frac{\text{Premium}}{\text{Strike Price}}$$

For this strategy, time is your friend since every passing day reduces the mathematical likelihood an out-of-the-money put goes in the money by expiration. At expiration, the value of the out-of-the-money put becomes zero.

The following example with Hecla Mining (HL) demonstrates the strategy. HL has been trading in the $10 to $8 range as shown in the chart below. The probability of HL falling below $8 in the next 30 to 60 days is less then 10% as provided by the Probability of Price Achievement table.

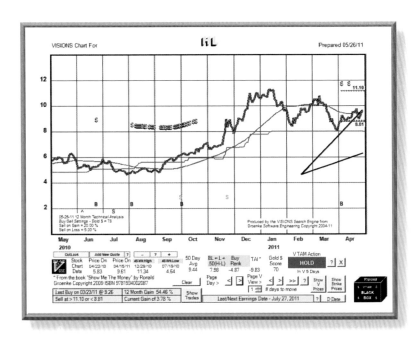

```
Probability of Price Achievement for HL on 05/03/11

Current Stock Price 8.42

    Probability in % Stock Price is Lower then Target

Target    <<< For these Days into the Future  >>>
Price      30      60     120     180     240     300
-----    ------  ------  ------  ------  ------  ------
  5       0.96    2.16    5.36   10.76   21.07    9.37
  6       2.98    6.71   16.65   33.44   63.30   78.81
  7       4.28    9.64   23.93   48.05   73.43   89.04
  8       4.48   10.10   25.07   50.44   74.68   89.56
  9      23.85   42.05   43.83   63.54   81.38   92.32
 10      98.70   97.07   82.63   84.43   92.05   96.72
 11      99.73   99.38   98.47   96.72   98.33   99.31
 12     100.00  100.00  100.00  100.00  100.00  100.00
```

The trade analysis is as follows: Selling an $8 put provides a short-term return of 1.81% with a probability of assignment of less then 5%. A slightly longer (46 days) trade provides a return of 3.94% with a probability of assignment of less than 10%. A shorter trade has a higher probability of success as indicated by the Probability of Price Achievement table. Anything beyond 120 days has a 25% or more chance of being assigned.

```
Naked Put for HL on 05/02/11 7:34 PM

Sell 10 HL May 20 2011 8.00 Puts @ 0.16              144.96
Prob of Assignment = 3.34%             Stock Price = 8.87
OTM 18 Days to Expiration                Put Value = 8000
Cash Covered Return =    144.96        1.81% (36.74 APR)
------------------------------------------------------------

Sell 10 HL Jun 17 2011 8.00 Puts @ 0.33              314.92
Prob of Assignment = 8.51%             Stock Price = 8.87
OTM 46 Days to Expiration                Put Value = 8000
Cash Covered Return =    314.92        3.94% (31.24 APR)
------------------------------------------------------------
```

To improve success when using naked puts, I have developed a formula that takes into account the premium, strike price, and time to expiration called the Put Factor. This number allows you to sort and filter Puts in order to narrow the search to just those that fit your criteria. It speeds up the selection process and allows you to spend more time analyzing the potential trades based on Probability of Assignment.

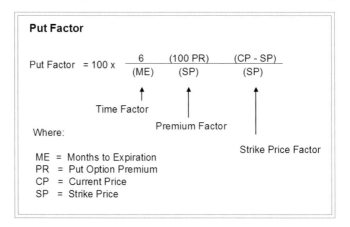

The Time Factor keeps the time to expiration short (for this factor to be high, months to expiration needs to be short). The number 6 keeps the months to expiration small. One month out gives a value of 6. Two months out a value of 3 and three months out a value of 2. That is why one month out is desirable providing a reasonable premium is available.

The Premium Factor selects the best percentage of premium to strike price (a small premium in relation to stock price is not desirable). You do not want to tie up real $ or margin for a premium that is not worth very much.

The Strike Price factor makes sure the strike price is not too close to the current stock price. If the strike price is greater than the current stock price, the Put Factor goes negative, which is not a good idea.

By multiplying these together you get the effect of each component. The multiplier (100) is used to get the value to a single digit if possible. When looking at Put Factor values, something close to or above 1 is desirable, since the right reward is achieved for the risk taken.

To learn more on how to invest using options I suggest you read my book *Show Me the Money—Covered Calls & Naked Puts for a Monthly Cash Income,* ISBN 9781934002087.

Here is an example of some put factor values for well known stocks.

Stock Symbl	Stock Price	Strike Date	Strike Price	Option Bid	Option Asked	Put Factor	Mths Till Exp	Prob of Asgnmt
-----	------	--------	------	-----	-----	------	----	------
AA	15.23	8/19/2011	14	0.36	0.38	**0.69**	1	8.31
BAC	10.52	8/19/2011	10	0.38	0.40	**0.60**	1	< 1.00
CAT	100	8/19/2011	90	1.83	1.86	**0.69**	1	8.69
JPM	39.49	8/19/2011	36	0.76	0.78	**0.63**	1	< 1.00
AXP	48.34	8/19/2011	45	1.04	1.07	**0.52**	1	11.90
CAT	100	8/19/2011	95	3.10	3.20	**0.53**	1	10.86
CSCO	14.93	8/19/2011	14	0.37	0.38	**0.54**	1	< 1.00
JPM	39.49	8/19/2011	37	1.00	1.02	**0.56**	1	< 1.00
BAC	10.52	9/16/2011	9	0.24	0.25	**0.91**	2	< 1.00
JPM	39.49	9/16/2011	35	0.84	0.87	**0.62**	2	< 1.00
BAC	10.52	9/16/2011	10	0.49	0.50	**0.52**	2	< 1.00
JPM	39.49	9/16/2011	36	1.06	1.08	**0.58**	2	< 1.00
BAC	10.52	10/21/2011	8	0.18	0.20	**1.01**	4	< 1.00
BAC	10.52	10/21/2011	9	0.34	0.36	**0.91**	4	< 1.00
AA	15.23	10/21/2011	12	0.27	0.28	**0.86**	4	12.50
AA	15.23	10/21/2011	13	0.45	0.47	**0.85**	4	16.47
JPM	39.49	10/21/2011	33	0.83	0.86	**0.70**	4	< 1.00
AXP	48.34	10/21/2011	40	0.85	0.89	**0.63**	4	4.76
AXP	48.34	10/21/2011	41	1.00	1.03	**0.62**	4	7.94
AXP	48.34	10/21/2011	42	1.17	1.20	**0.60**	4	11.71
JPM	39.49	10/21/2011	35	1.24	1.27	**0.65**	4	< 1.00
AXP	48.34	10/21/2011	43	1.27	1.41	**0.52**	4	17.86
CSCO	14.93	10/21/2011	13	0.35	0.37	**0.57**	4	< 1.00
DD	51.96	10/21/2011	45	1.05	1.08	**0.51**	4	13.10
DD	51.96	10/21/2011	46	1.24	1.27	**0.50**	4	14.68
GE	17.97	10/21/2011	15	0.31	0.32	**0.58**	4	4.17
GE	17.97	10/21/2011	16	0.48	0.49	**0.53**	4	9.92
INTC	21.2	10/21/2011	18	0.37	0.38	**0.52**	4	< 1.00
JPM	39.49	10/21/2011	36	1.50	1.54	**0.58**	4	< 1.00

Double Up

"Anyone who has never made a mistake has never tried anything new."

Albert Einstein

STRATEGY: Buy a stock, sell a call at-the-money or slightly out-of-the-money and sell a put at a lower strike price with a low probability of assignment.

OUTLOOK: Expecting the stock to trade in a channel such that the call is assigned and the put expires worthless. If both the call and put expire, sell another call and put a month out for income generation. If the call expires and the put is assigned, sell calls on the full position. If the call is assigned, review this or another candidate for a new covered call and naked put opportunity.

PROFIT: If the call and put expire, the return is the call and put option premium received. If the call is assigned, the return is the call and put option premium plus any price appreciation in the stock that is limited by the strike price of the call sold.

RISK: Risk is related to stock ownership. It is reduced by the amount of the call and put option premium received. Worst case is stock goes to zero. To exit this trade, buy the call back to close and sell the stock. Wait for put expiration or sell the position when assigned.

BREAK EVEN: Stock purchase price less the call and put option premiums received.

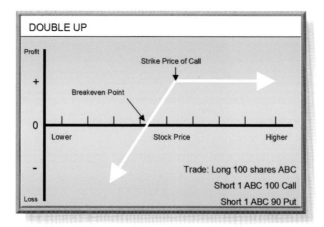

This strategy is a combination of a covered call and a naked put. It provides a way to generate excellent returns while building a stock portfolio with good companies. This trade needs to be monitored and may need action in case something bad happens to the stock price.

You can apply this strategy at any time, but I find it most useful when investing in a new good company for the first time. Let's say you were planning to commit $20,000 to an investment. You can invest it all up front and buy 2000 shares at $10 per share and write a covered call. If the stock does not perform as expected you might have unnecessarily increased the risk. Why not reduce the risk by buying half of our desired position now for the covered call and sell a put at a strike price below the current price of the stock? Now if the stock goes down before the put expires we will buy our full commitment with an overall lower entry price. If the put expires, the return on our initial position is enhanced by the value of the put premium received. If this is done in a margin account, the value of the first commitment can be used as the margin for the put sold. However, caution must be used in the level of margin committed in the account. Limiting the use of margin to about 40% of the margin available can usually sustain severe market corrections.

After experiencing a number of option cycles with the new stock, one can move to a full covered call strategy.

This strategy can be repeated over and over when a stock or ETF trades in a channel or small range. For example, buy at $15.50; sell a call at $16 and a put at $15. If the stock does not move much you continue with a new call and put in the channel range. If the stock moves up, you implement a call and put in the new range. If the stock moves down, you usually can sell calls at the lower strike price and still generate an acceptable return. This gives you a positive return on the investment, even when the price of the stock goes down.

The example, which follows, demonstrates this strategy with the Home Builder (XHB) ETF. It has traded in a number of different channels over a 12-month period.

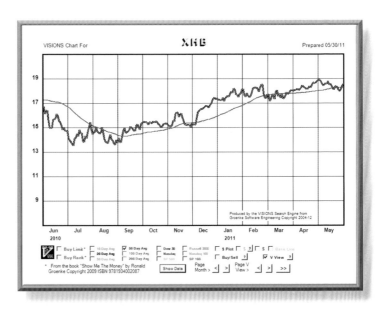

XHB was in the $17 to $18 channel for over 3 months. Now it is in the $18 to $19 channel. It is a prime candidate for a call at $19 and a put at $18. The following trade provides an overall return of 1.74% in 46 days if both the call and put expire. The probability of the call being assigned is 7.38% and the probability of the put being assigned is 11.97%. This suggests that XHB is range bound for some time.

```
Double Up for XHB on 05/30/11 3:47 PM

Buy 1000 XHB @ 18.70                             -18705.00
Sell 10 XHB Jul 15 2011 19.00 Calls @ 0.39         374.90
Prob of Assignment = 7.38%       Called Value = 18975.33
OTM 46 Days to Expiration          Breakeven = 18330.10
If Sold Gain    =     645.23            3.45% (27.37 APR)
If Expired Gain =     374.90            2.00% (15.90 APR)

Sell 10 XHB Jul 15 2011 18.00 Puts @ 0.28          264.93
Prob of Assignment = 11.97%        Stock Price = 18.70
OTM 46 Days to Expiration            Put Value = 18000
Cash Covered Return =     264.93       1.47% (11.68 APR)
------------------ Double Up Return -------------------
Call & Put Exp Gain          639.83    1.74% (13.83 APR)
Call Asgnd & Put Exp Gain    910.16    2.48% (19.68 APR)
-------------------------------------------------------
```

If we move to September options, our return goes up, but is less then 2.37 (109/46) times the July options. This again shows that the option premium curve is non-linear. If the September call and put expire, the return is 3.81% in 109 days, for an annualized return of 12.77%. The probability of the call being assigned has gone down to 2.61%. The probability of the put being assigned has gone up to 47.67%. This demonstrates the nature of the risk in a naked put. Lots of things can happen in a longer time frame. For this reason, the shorter time frame July options are desirable. It gives us the opportunity to make a new decision on what to do next in 47 days. We also have the opportunity to pick up the higher premium values. The Walk the Talk chapter provides additional detail on a number of XHB trades that shows this Double Up trade strategy.

```
Double Up for XHB on 05/30/11 3:47 PM

Buy 1000 XHB @ 18.70                             -18705.00
Sell 10 XHB Sep 16 2011 19.00 Calls @ 0.77         754.81
Prob of Assignment = 2.61%       Called Value = 18975.33
OTM 109 Days to Expiration         Breakeven = 17950.19
If Sold Gain    =    1025.14           5.48% (18.35 APR)
If Expired Gain =     754.81           4.04% (13.51 APR)

Sell 10 XHB Sep 16 2011 18.00 Puts @ 0.66          644.83
Prob of Assignment = 47.64%        Stock Price = 18.70
OTM 109 Days to Expiration           Put Value = 18000
Cash Covered Return =     644.83       3.58% (12.00 APR)
------------------ Double Up Return -------------------
Call & Put Exp Gain         1399.64    3.81% (12.77 APR)
Call Asgnd & Put Exp Gain   1669.97    4.55% (15.24 APR)
-------------------------------------------------------
```

Fence

"Attitude is a little thing that makes a big difference."
Winston Churchill

STRATEGY: Buy a stock, sell a slightly out-of-the-money call, and buy a put at a lower strike price with a low probability of assignment.

OUTLOOK: Expecting the stock to trade in a channel such that the call is assigned and the put expires worthless. If both the call and put expire, sell another call and buy a put a month out for income generation. If the call expires and the put is in the money put (sell) the stock. If the call is assigned, review this or another candidate for a new Fence opportunity.

PROFIT: If the call and put expire, the return is the call less the put option premium for the put purchased. If the call is assigned, the return is the call less the put option premium plus any price appreciation in the stock that is limited by the strike price of the call sold.

RISK: Risk is related to stock ownership. It is reduced by the amount of the call less the put option premium received. Worst case is stock goes to zero. To exit this trade, wait until expiration day and put (sell) the position. The call will expire worthless.

BREAK EVEN: Stock purchase price plus put premium less the call option premium received.

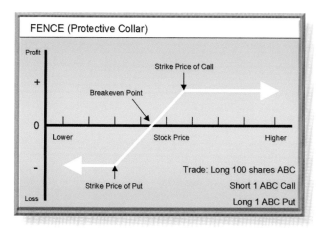

This trade is very conservative. You buy or own a position in a stock and buy a put to protect any downside. You sell a call to help pay for the protection. Both the upside and downside are closed off or fenced in.

The put option added to the stock position insures the stock's value. The choice of strike prices determines the level of downside protection. You get the benefit of upside gains up to the strike price of the call sold.

Here are three Fence alternatives for review. If we want to optimize the return, the $30 put looks like the right choice. Buying a $32 put does not add much to the protection. The probability the price is less than $32 is 11.45% versus 11.20% for the $30 put. Buying a $34 put provides the greatest protection but also reduces the return. It all depends on your view for the price of silver in the near term and your willingness to take on risk. I would be comfortable with the $30 put, since it protects one from a crash in the silver price. If the price does go down somewhat, the opportunity to recover by selling future calls is always an alternative.

FENCE Example

```
Fence (Protective Collar) for GE on 06/30/11 9:21 PM

Buy 1000 GE @ 18.86                              -18865.00
Sell 10 GE Aug 19 2011 20.00 Calls @ 0.16          144.96
Buy 10 GE Aug 19 2011 16.00 Puts @ 0.09           -105.00
Stock Price = 18.86                 Breakeven = 18.79
Probability Price > or = 20.00 in 51 Days =        12.74 %
Probability Price < or = 16.00 in 51 Days =         3.24 %
-------------------- Fence Return --------------------
Call Asgnd & Put Exp Gain      1150.26   6.10% (43.64 APR)
Call & Put Exp Gain              39.96   0.21% (1.52 APR)
------------------------------------------------------


Fence (Protective Collar) for BA on 06/30/11 10:29 PM

Buy 1000 BA @ 73.93                              -73935.00
Sell 10 BA Aug 19 2011 77.50 Calls @ 0.89          874.78
Buy 10 BA Aug 19 2011 67.50 Puts @ 0.78           -795.00
Stock Price = 73.93                 Breakeven = 73.82
Probability Price > or = 77.50 in 51 Days =        20.61 %
Probability Price < or = 67.50 in 51 Days =         6.55 %
-------------------- Fence Return --------------------
Call Asgnd & Put Exp Gain      3606.31   4.88% (34.91 APR)
Call & Put Exp Gain              79.78   0.11% (0.77 APR)
------------------------------------------------------


Fence (Protective Collar) for MMM on 06/30/11 9:21 PM

Buy 1000 MMM @ 94.85                             -94855.00
Sell 10 MMM Aug 19 2011 97.50 Calls @ 1.17        1154.71
Buy 10 MMM Aug 19 2011 85.00 Puts @ 0.44          -455.00
Stock Price = 94.85                 Breakeven = 94.12
Probability Price > or = 97.50 in 51 Days =       < 1.00 %
Probability Price < or = 85.00 in 51 Days =         3.88 %
-------------------- Fence Return --------------------
Call Asgnd & Put Exp Gain      3301.01   3.48% (24.91 APR)
Call & Put Exp Gain             699.71   0.74% (5.28 APR)
------------------------------------------------------


Fence (Protective Collar) for JPM on 06/30/11 10:26 PM

Buy 1000 JPM @ 40.94                             -40945.00
Sell 10 JPM Aug 19 2011 42.00 Calls @ 0.94         924.76
Buy 10 JPM Aug 19 2011 37.00 Puts @ 0.48          -495.00
Stock Price = 40.94                 Breakeven = 40.48
Probability Price > or = 42.00 in 51 Days =        42.38 %
Probability Price < or = 37.00 in 51 Days =       < 1.00 %
-------------------- Fence Return --------------------
Call Asgnd & Put Exp Gain      1454.54   3.55% (25.42 APR)
Call & Put Exp Gain             429.76   1.05% (7.51 APR)
------------------------------------------------------
```

Married Put

"Facts are stubborn things."

Ronald Reagan

STRATEGY: Buy a stock and buy a put at a strike price with a low probability of assignment for downside protection.

OUTLOOK: Expecting the stock to trade up such that the put expires worthless.

PROFIT: The return is the price appreciation in the stock less the cost of the put.

RISK: Risk is limited to the stock purchase price less the strike price of the put. To exit this trade, wait until expiration day and put (sell) the position.

BREAK EVEN: Stock purchase price plus put premium.

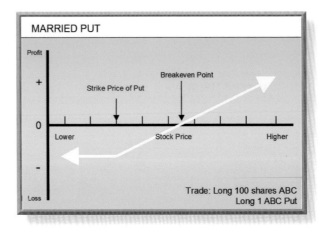

This is a hedge trade. You buy or own a position in a stock and buy a put to protect any downside.

The put option added to the stock position insures the stock's value. The choice of strike prices determines the level of downside protection. If the stock stays strong, you still get the benefit of upside gains. If there is a short-term up trend before the put expires, it could be sold back to recover some of its cost. But if the stock falls below the strike, as originally feared, you have several choices. One is to exercise the put, which triggers the sale of the stock. The strike price sets the minimum exit price. If the long-term outlook has turned bearish, this could be the most prudent move.

The put can provide excellent protection against a major downturn during the term of the option. The one drawback of this strategy is its cost. The stock must appreciate enough to cover the cost of the put purchased and the purchase price of the stock to become a successful investment. This is the main difference when compared to the Fence strategy where a call is sold to help pay for the purchase of the put.

Insurance costs money so the decision here is to determine how much insurance to buy and for how long. The following table shows that the probability of AXP being below 42 in 187 days is about 43% (probability it is above 42 is 100–43 or 57%). Insurance at this level is $2005 or about 4.4% of the current price. It might be a good decision if there is a feeling that the stock could be under stress or a market correction is near.

MARRIED PUT Example

```
Married Put for AAPL on 06/30/11 8:15 PM

Buy 1000 AAPL @ 335.67                      -335675.00
Buy 10 AAPL Jul 15 2011 305.00 Puts @ 0.37     -385.00
Probability Price < or = 305.00 in 16 Days =     1.66 %
Probability Price > or = 355.00 in 16 Days =   < 1.00 %
Return at 355.00 = 18836.09          5.61% (128.01 APR)
----------------------------------------------------------

Married Put for AXP on 06/30/11 8:15 PM

Buy 1000 AXP @ 51.70                         -51705.00
Buy 10 AXP Jul 15 2011 47.50 Puts @ 0.12       -135.00
Probability Price < or = 47.50 in 16 Days =     11.74 %
Probability Price > or = 55.00 in 16 Days =    < 1.00 %
Return at 55.00 = 3127.08             6.05% (137.97 APR)
----------------------------------------------------------

Married Put for GOOG on 06/30/11 8:15 PM

Buy 1000 GOOG @ 506.38                      -506385.00
Buy 10 GOOG Jul 15 2011 465.00 Puts @ 2.75    -2765.00
Probability Price < or = 465.00 in 16 Days =   < 1.00 %
Probability Price > or = 535.00 in 16 Days =     3.07 %
Return at 535.00 = 25703.41           5.08% (115.79 APR)
----------------------------------------------------------

Married Put for INTC on 06/30/11 5:04 PM

Buy 1000 INTC @ 22.16                        -22165.00
Buy 10 INTC Aug 19 2011 20.00 Puts @ 0.22      -235.00
Probability Price < or = 20.00 in 51 Days =      4.86 %
Probability Price > or = 24.00 in 51 Days =    < 1.00 %
Return at 24.00 = 1574.47             7.10% (50.84 APR)
----------------------------------------------------------

Married Put for GG on 06/30/11 9:17 PM

Buy 1000 GG @ 48.27                          -48275.00
Buy 10 GG Jul 15 2011 44.00 Puts @ 0.14        -155.00
Probability Price < or = 44.00 in 16 Days =      2.09 %
Probability Price > or = 52.50 in 16 Days =    < 1.00 %
Return at 52.50 = 4037.94             8.36% (190.81 APR)
----------------------------------------------------------
```

Open Fence

"If you can dream it, you can do it."

Walt Disney

STRATEGY: Sell a call and a put on a stock that is trading in a channel.

OUTLOOK: Expecting the stock to trade sideways such that both the call and put expire worthless.

PROFIT: The maximum gain occurs if the underlying stock remains between the strike prices. In that case, both options expire worthless and the gain is the premium received for selling the options. If the call is close to being in the money, buy a position to cover or move it out in time and up to avoid assignment. If the put is close to assignment, move it out in time and down in strike price to avoid assignment.

RISK: Risk is related to stock ownership. If the put is assigned, the purchase price is reduced by the amount of the put and call option premiums received. Worst case is stock goes to zero. To exit this trade, buy to close the option that is in the money and let the other option expire worthless.

BREAK EVEN: Call Strike price plus all option premiums received, or Put Strike price less all option premiums received.

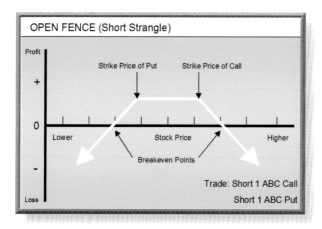

This strategy is used when you have found a stock that trades in a channel for long periods of time. It allows you to capitalize on little or no price movement and earn income from selling premiums. To succeed, pick out-of-the-money strike prices that have a 5–8% or lower probability of assignment establishing a trading range that fits the pattern of the last fifty days. This strategy is really a race between volatility and time decay. Volatility is the storm, which might blow in at any moment and cause extreme losses. The passage of time is a constant that every day brings you a little closer to realizing your expected gain.

This strategy is considered to have very high risk and limited reward. Do not use this strategy if you do not have the assets available to buy the position to cover the call or an assignment of the put. This trade needs to be monitored and may need action in case the stock has a significant up or down movement.

Think of this as a fence that is open at the top and the bottom. You need to watch what is behind the fence to make sure it does not get out at the top (stock price goes up) or goes out the bottom (stock price goes down). If the stock price gets close to the call strike price, buy the position to cover or roll it up and out. If the price gets close to the put strike, roll the put out and down. At expiration, if the price is above the upper opening the call is assigned and you get to make a new decision. If the price is below the lower opening, the call will expire and you now get to write another out of money call. For each option cycle period you are guaranteed that one option will expire worthless.

Here are some ground rules for an Open Fence strategy.

You need cash in your account to cover the highest assignment (strike price x number of shares). For retirement accounts you will need cash to cover both the call and put.

You want to sell short-term (3 to 4 weeks) puts and calls that have a low probability of assignment. For puts, a P of A that is less then 5%, and for calls, a P of A less then 8%.

Track the stock prices every day. Be ready to act and do not procrastinate. Discipline is very important. You do not want the stock price to move up through the call strike without taking action. Do the same on the down side. In most cases you will be able to preserve all premiums earned and even add to the total. The market is not forgiving.

Stay away from of any situation where a stock is involved in a restructuring or capitalization event. Some examples might be a merger, takeover, spin-off or special dividend. This could completely upset typical expectations and cause early exercise of options on the stock.

The maximum loss does not have a limit and occurs when the stock dramatically decreases or increases away from the current strike prices. The potential maximum gain for this strategy is limited to the net credit initially received for the put and call option. In this strategy, time decay is the option trader's friend. With a passage in time, all other things being equal, will result in a decrease in option premiums and help the strategy achieve its full profit potential.

This strategy breaks even if, at expiration, the stock price is either above the call strike price or below the put strike price by the amount of the total premium received. At either of those levels, one options intrinsic value will equal the premium received for selling both options while the other option will be expiring worthless.

Four Open Fence examples are provided for review.

The first example is for the Silver ETF (SLV). This ETF invests in silver and allows one to participate in the silver trade without taking ownership of the physical metal. The trades selected provide about a 3% return when silver stays in the $32 to $39 range. The probability that silver trades outside this range is less then 10% on the low side and around 1% on the high side. The risk is you need to buy silver if it gets above $39 or take assignment at $32. Since this ETF tracks silver, you can make your decision based on your view of where silver trades the next 45 days. The following chart shows that the selected range should be very successful.

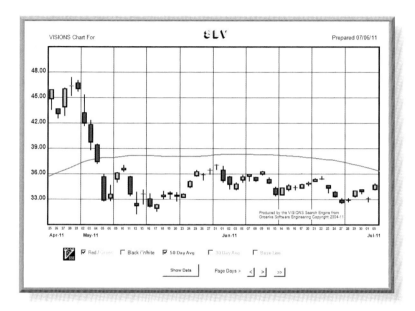

The second example is Apple (AAPL). This is the stock that was shown early on that had a run up during the 2009–10 recession. The return with an Open Fence on this stock is very low. The reason for that is that to reduce the risk of assignment, the range becomes such, that the option premiums available are lower then wanted. Why take the risk for the minimal return?

```
Open Fence (Short Strangle) for SLV      07/06/11 11:51 AM

Sell 10 SLV Aug 19 2011 39.00 Calls @ 0.53          514.87
Sell 10 SLV Aug 19 2011 32.00 Puts  @ 0.62          604.84
Stock Price = 35.30          Breakeven = 30.85 or 37.85
Probability Price > or = 39.00 in 45 Days =           1.02 %
Probability Price < or = 32.00 in 45 Days =           9.57 %
Call Value = 39000.00              Put Value = 32000.00
----------------- Open Fence Return -----------------
Call & Put Exp Gain          1119.71    3.15% (25.58 APR)
Call Asgnd & Put Exp Gain    1119.71    2.87% (23.29 APR)
Put Asgnd & Call Exp Gain    1119.71    3.50% (28.38 APR)
-----------------------------------------------------


Open Fence (Short Strangle) for AAPL   07/06/11 11:50 AM

Sell 10 AAPL Aug 19 2011 390.00 Calls @ 1.80      1784.55
Sell 10 AAPL Aug 19 2011 290.00 Puts  @ 0.68       664.83
Stock Price = 350.94         Breakeven = 287.52 or 387.52
Probability Price > or = 390.00 in 45 Days =      < 1.00 %
Probability Price < or = 290.00 in 45 Days =        3.83 %
Call Value = 390000.00            Put Value = 290000.00
----------------- Open Fence Return -------------------
Call & Put Exp Gain          2449.38    0.72% (5.84 APR)
Call Asgnd & Put Exp Gain    2449.38    0.63% (5.09 APR)
Put Asgnd & Call Exp Gain    2449.38    0.84% (6.85 APR)
-----------------------------------------------------


Open Fence (Short Strangle) for AXP      07/06/11 11:52 AM

Sell 10 AXP Aug 19 2011 57.50 Calls @ 0.20          184.95
Sell 10 AXP Aug 19 2011 40.00 Puts  @ 0.08           64.98
Stock Price = 52.23          Breakeven = 39.72 or 57.22
Probability Price > or = 57.50 in 45 Days =      < 1.00 %
Probability Price < or = 40.00 in 45 Days =        1.61 %
Call Value = 57500.00              Put Value = 40000.00
----------------- Open Fence Return -------------------
Call & Put Exp Gain           249.93    0.51% (4.16 APR)
Call Asgnd & Put Exp Gain     249.93    0.43% (3.53 APR)
Put Asgnd & Call Exp Gain     249.93    0.62% (5.07 APR)
-----------------------------------------------------


Open Fence (Short Strangle) for UCO      07/06/11 11:53 AM

Sell 10 UCO Aug 19 2011 51.00 Calls @ 0.65          634.84
Sell 10 UCO Aug 19 2011 38.00 Puts  @ 1.15         1134.71
Stock Price = 43.77          Breakeven = 36.20 or 49.20
Probability Price > or = 51.00 in 45 Days =         2.75 %
Probability Price < or = 38.00 in 45 Days =         1.91 %
Call Value = 51000.00              Put Value = 38000.00
----------------- Open Fence Return -------------------
Call & Put Exp Gain          1769.55    3.98% (32.25 APR)
Call Asgnd & Put Exp Gain    1769.55    3.47% (28.14 APR)
Put Asgnd & Call Exp Gain    1769.55    4.66% (37.77 APR)
-----------------------------------------------------
```

The next example is with American Express (AXP). The potential return, again, is somewhat low, caused by the large range selected to reduce the possibility of assignment. The chart provided below with AXP outlook, shows AXP could jump up significantly and force a *buy to cover* to limit the upside risk. Again, why take the risk for the limited return?

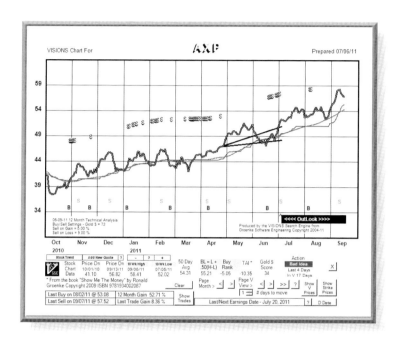

The final example is with the 2X Oil ETF (UCO). The investment seeks to provide daily investment results (before fees and expenses) that correspond to twice the daily performance of the Dow Jones UBS Crude Oil Sub-Index. The fund invests primarily in any one of or combinations of Financial Instruments, including swap agreements, futures contracts, and options on futures contracts or forward contracts with respect to the applicable benchmark, to the extent determined appropriate by the Sponsor. This is somewhat like the silver example. Here you invest in oil without taking delivery. If oil stays in the $90 to $100 range (price of oil at this time) this trade can be repeated over and over. The wider the range the lower the risk and total premiums received. Another point to consider is that the price of oil will not go to zero.

Bull/Bear Spreads

"Believe you can and you're halfway there."

Theodore Roosevelt

A spread is an options strategy that requires two actions that you execute at the same time. You purchase one option and sell another option on the same stock or ETF. Both options are identical except for the strike price. This results in a vertical spread, in which one option has a higher strike price than the other. The SPREAD is the difference between the higher strike price and the lower strike price.

Different spread strategies are used for different stocks and general market direction or forecast. You use a BEAR spread if you think the direction is down and BULL spread if you think the direction is up. To be successful you need to pick the correct direction of the stock move, which could also be influenced by general market conditions during the period.

The first step in executing a spread is selecting the underlying equity or ETF on which to purchase and sell options. The next step is to choose the strike prices and strike date. This includes determining how much you think the stock will move and how long it will take to do so. Then you calculate the maximum profit, maximum loss, and breakeven for the strategy. This sets the bounds on the returns that can be expected and allows you to establish an exit point.

The four most common vertical spread strategies that can be implemented are provided with trade examples.

Bull Put Credit Spread.

STRATEGY: Buy a put at a lower strike price and sell a put at a higher strike price.

OUTLOOK: Expecting a neutral to bullish market with an increase in the price of the underlying security above the strike price of the put option sold.

PROFIT: Limited to the net credit received. Profit is achieved when the underlying security closes above the strike price of the put sold. This is a credit trade when initiated.

RISK: Risk is limited to the difference in strike prices times the number of shares less the net credit.

BREAK EVEN: Strike price of the higher put minus the net credit received.

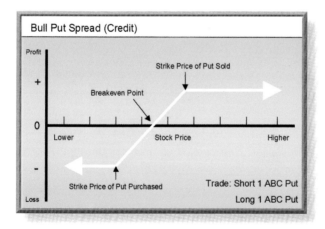

85

Bear Put Debit Spread

STRATEGY: Buy a put at a higher strike price and sell a put at a lower strike price.

OUTLOOK: Expecting a neutral to bearish market with a decrease in the price of the underlying security below the strike price of the put option sold.

PROFIT: Equal to difference in strike prices times the number of shares less the net debit paid. Maximum profit results when the underlying security closes at or below the strike price of the put sold.

RISK: Risk is limited to the net debit paid for the spread. Maximum risk results when the underlying security closes at or above the strike price of the put purchased.

BREAK EVEN: Strike price of the higher put minus the net debit paid.

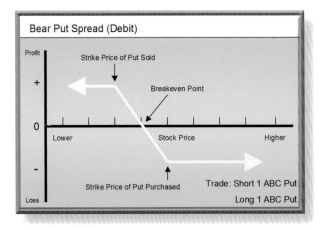

Bull Call Debit Spread

STRATEGY: Buy a call at a lower strike price and sell a call at a higher strike price.

OUTLOOK: Expecting a flat to Bullish market with an increase in the price of the underlying security above the strike price of the call option sold.

PROFIT: Equal to difference in strike prices times number of shares less the debit incurred (Premium of call purchased less premium of call sold). Maximum profit results when the underlying security closes above the strike price of the call sold.

RISK: Risk is limited to the net debit paid for the spread. Maximum risk results when the underlying security closes at or below the strike price of the call purchased.

BREAK EVEN: Strike price of the call sold, less the per share debit incurred.

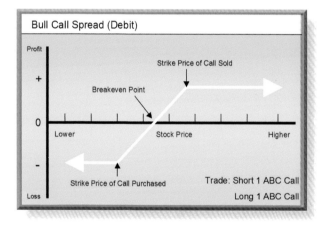

Bear Call Credit Spread

STRATEGY: Buy a call at a higher strike price and sell a call at a lower strike price.

OUTLOOK: Expecting a Bearish market and a decrease in the price of the underlying security below the strike price of the call option sold.

PROFIT: Limited to the credit received (Premium of call sold less premium of call purchased). Maximum profit results when the underlying security closes below the strike price of the call sold.

RISK: Risk is limited to the difference in strike prices times number of shares, less the credit received. Maximum risk results when the underlying security closes at or above the strike price of the call purchased.

BREAK EVEN: It is the Strike price of the call sold, plus the per share credit received.

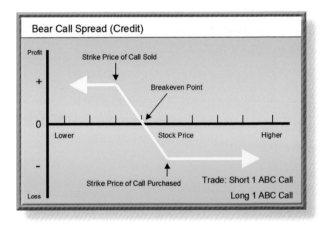

```
Bull Put Spread for AMZN               11/18/11 8:33 PM

Sell 10 AMZN Dec 16 2011 195.00 Puts @ 8.65      8632.84
Buy  10 AMZN Dec 16 2011 190.00 Puts @ 6.75     -6765.00
Probability Price > or = 195.00 in 29 Days =      94.69 %
Probability Price < or = 190.00 in 29 Days =       4.59 %
------------ Bull Put Credit Spread Return -------------
Maximum Gain = 1867.84 (37.36%)   at price > or = 195.00
Maximum Loss = 3132.16 (62.64%)   at price < or = 190.00
Breakeven = 193.13           Current Stock Price = 197.14
----------------------------------------------------------

Bear Put Spread for AMZN               11/18/11 8:33 PM

Buy  10 AMZN Dec 16 2011 195.00 Puts @ 8.80     -8815.00
Sell 10 AMZN Dec 16 2011 190.00 Puts @ 6.65      6633.34
Probability Price > or = 195.00 in 29 Days =      94.69 %
Probability Price < or = 190.00 in 29 Days =       4.59 %
------------ Bear Put Debit Spread Return -------------
Maximum Gain = 2818.34 (56.37%)   at price < or = 190.00
Maximum Loss = 2181.66 (43.63%)   at price > or = 195.00
Breakeven = 192.82           Current Stock Price = 197.14
----------------------------------------------------------

Bull Call Spread for AMZN              11/18/11 8:29 PM

Sell 10 AMZN Nov 25 2011 200.00 Calls @ 3.55     3534.11
Buy  10 AMZN Nov 25 2011 190.00 Calls @ 9.75    -9765.00
Probability Price > or = 200.00 in 8 Days =       97.96 %
Probability Price < or = 190.00 in 8 Days =        1.57 %
------------ Bull Call Debit Spread Return -------------
Maximum Gain = 3769.11 (37.69%)   at price > or = 200.00
Maximum Loss = 6230.89 (62.31%)   at price < or = 190.00
Breakeven = 196.23           Current Stock Price = 197.14
----------------------------------------------------------

Bear Call Spread for AMZN              11/18/11 8:29 PM

Buy  10 AMZN Nov 25 2011 200.00 Calls @ 3.65    -3665.00
Sell 10 AMZN Nov 25 2011 190.00 Calls @ 9.40     9382.65
Probability Price > or = 200.00 in 8 Days =       97.96 %
Probability Price < or = 190.00 in 8 Days =        1.57 %
------------ Bear Call Credit Spread Return -------------
Maximum Gain = 5717.65 (57.18%)   at price < or = 190.00
Maximum Loss = 4282.35 (42.82%)   at price > or = 200.00
Breakeven = 195.72           Current Stock Price = 197.14
----------------------------------------------------------
```

```
Bull Put Spread for BP                    11/18/11 8:33 PM

Sell 10 BP Dec 16 2011 42.00 Puts @ 1.28          1264.68
Buy  10 BP Dec 16 2011 40.00 Puts @ 0.73          -745.00
Probability Price > or = 42.00 in 29 Days =        80.26 %
Probability Price < or = 40.00 in 29 Days =         2.09 %
------------ Bull Put Credit Spread Return -------------
Maximum Gain = 519.68 (25.98%)     at price > or = 42.00
Maximum Loss = 1480.32 (74.02%)    at price < or = 40.00
Breakeven = 41.48            Current Stock Price = 42.48
---------------------------------------------------------


Bear Put Spread for BP                    11/18/11 8:33 PM

Buy  10 BP Dec 16 2011 42.00 Puts @ 1.31         -1325.00
Sell 10 BP Dec 16 2011 40.00 Puts @ 0.71           694.82
Probability Price > or = 42.00 in 29 Days =        80.26 %
Probability Price < or = 40.00 in 29 Days =         2.09 %
------------ Bear Put Debit Spread Return -------------
Maximum Gain = 1369.82 (68.49%)    at price < or = 40.00
Maximum Loss = 630.18 (31.51%)     at price > or = 42.00
Breakeven = 41.37            Current Stock Price = 42.48
---------------------------------------------------------


Bull Call Spread for BP                   11/18/11 8:29 PM

Sell 10 BP Nov 25 2011 43.00 Calls @ 0.41          394.90
Buy  10 BP Nov 25 2011 41.00 Calls @ 1.77        -1785.00
Probability Price > or = 43.00 in 8 Days =         74.28 %
Probability Price < or = 41.00 in 8 Days =          0.85 %
------------ Bull Call Debit Spread Return -------------
Maximum Gain = 609.90 (30.50%)     at price > or = 43.00
Maximum Loss = 1390.10 (69.51%)    at price < or = 41.00
Breakeven = 42.39            Current Stock Price = 42.48
---------------------------------------------------------


Bear Call Spread for BP                   11/18/11 8:29 PM

Buy  10 BP Nov 25 2011 43.00 Calls @ 0.46         -475.00
Sell 10 BP Nov 25 2011 41.00 Calls @ 1.69         1674.58
Probability Price > or = 43.00 in 8 Days =         74.28 %
Probability Price < or = 41.00 in 8 Days =          0.85 %
------------ Bear Call Credit Spread Return -------------
Maximum Gain = 1199.58 (59.98%)    at price < or = 41.00
Maximum Loss = 800.42 (40.02%)     at price > or = 43.00
Breakeven = 42.20            Current Stock Price = 42.48
---------------------------------------------------------
```

```
Bull Put Spread for GLD                    11/18/11 8:31 PM

Sell 10 GLD Dec 16 2011 165.00 Puts @ 3.25        3234.19
Buy  10 GLD Dec 16 2011 160.00 Puts @ 1.79       -1805.00
Probability Price > or = 165.00 in 29 Days =       75.93 %
Probability Price < or = 160.00 in 29 Days =       19.39 %
------------ Bull Put Credit Spread Return -------------
Maximum Gain = 1429.19 (28.58%)   at price > or = 165.00
Maximum Loss = 3570.81 (71.42%)   at price < or = 160.00
Breakeven = 163.57          Current Stock Price = 167.62
--------------------------------------------------------


Bear Put Spread for GLD                    11/18/11 8:31 PM

Buy  10 GLD Dec 16 2011 165.00 Puts @ 3.30       -3315.00
Sell 10 GLD Dec 16 2011 160.00 Puts @ 1.75        1734.56
Probability Price > or = 165.00 in 29 Days =       75.93 %
Probability Price < or = 160.00 in 29 Days =       19.39 %
------------ Bear Put Debit Spread Return -------------
Maximum Gain = 3419.56 (68.39%)   at price < or = 160.00
Maximum Loss = 1580.44 (31.61%)   at price > or = 165.00
Breakeven = 163.42          Current Stock Price = 167.62
--------------------------------------------------------


Bull Call Spread for GLD                   11/18/11 8:27 PM

Sell 10 GLD Nov 25 2011 168.00 Calls @ 1.74       1724.56
Buy  10 GLD Nov 25 2011 163.00 Calls @ 5.40      -5415.00
Probability Price > or = 168.00 in 8 Days =        85.22 %
Probability Price < or = 163.00 in 8 Days =         2.58 %
------------ Bull Call Debit Spread Return -------------
Maximum Gain = 1309.56 (26.19%)   at price > or = 168.00
Maximum Loss = 3690.44 (73.81%)   at price < or = 163.00
Breakeven = 166.69          Current Stock Price = 167.62
--------------------------------------------------------


Bear Call Spread for GLD                   11/18/11 8:27 PM

Buy  10 GLD Nov 25 2011 168.00 Calls @ 1.80      -1815.00
Sell 10 GLD Nov 25 2011 163.00 Calls @ 4.95       4933.76
Probability Price > or = 168.00 in 8 Days =        85.22 %
Probability Price < or = 163.00 in 8 Days =         2.58 %
------------ Bear Call Credit Spread Return -------------
Maximum Gain = 3118.76 (62.38%)   at price < or = 163.00
Maximum Loss = 1881.24 (37.62%)   at price > or = 168.00
Breakeven = 166.12          Current Stock Price = 167.62
--------------------------------------------------------
```

```
Bull Put Spread for FAS                      11/18/11 8:31 PM

Sell 10 FAS Dec 16 2011 58.00 Puts @ 6.80           6783.30
Buy  10 FAS Dec 16 2011 55.00 Puts @ 5.60          -5615.00
Probability Price > or = 58.00 in 29 Days =          95.40 %
Probability Price < or = 55.00 in 29 Days =         < 1.00 %
------------ Bull Put Credit Spread Return -------------
Maximum Gain = 1168.30 (38.94%)     at price > or = 58.00
Maximum Loss = 1831.70 (61.06%)     at price < or = 55.00
Breakeven = 56.83              Current Stock Price = 58.49
-------------------------------------------------------


Bear Put Spread for FAS                      11/18/11 8:31 PM

Buy  10 FAS Dec 16 2011 58.00 Puts @ 6.95          -6965.00
Sell 10 FAS Dec 16 2011 55.00 Puts @ 5.50           5483.62
Probability Price > or = 58.00 in 29 Days =          95.40 %
Probability Price < or = 55.00 in 29 Days =         < 1.00 %
------------ Bear Put Debit Spread Return -------------
Maximum Gain = 1518.62 (50.62%)     at price < or = 55.00
Maximum Loss = 1481.38 (49.38%)     at price > or = 58.00
Breakeven = 56.52              Current Stock Price = 58.49
-------------------------------------------------------


Bull Call Spread for FAS                     11/18/11 8:27 PM

Sell 10 FAS Nov 25 2011 59.00 Calls @ 2.64          2624.34
Buy  10 FAS Nov 25 2011 56.00 Calls @ 4.60         -4615.00
Probability Price > or = 59.00 in 8 Days =           87.71 %
Probability Price < or = 56.00 in 8 Days =            0.10 %
------------ Bull Call Debit Spread Return -------------
Maximum Gain = 1009.34 (33.64%)     at price > or = 59.00
Maximum Loss = 1990.66 (66.36%)     at price < or = 56.00
Breakeven = 57.99              Current Stock Price = 58.49
-------------------------------------------------------


Bear Call Spread for FAS                     11/18/11 8:27 PM

Buy  10 FAS Nov 25 2011 59.00 Calls @ 2.80         -2815.00
Sell 10 FAS Nov 25 2011 56.00 Calls @ 4.40          4383.90
Probability Price > or = 59.00 in 8 Days =           87.71 %
Probability Price < or = 56.00 in 8 Days =            0.10 %
------------ Bear Call Credit Spread Return -------------
Maximum Gain = 1568.90 (52.30%)     at price < or = 56.00
Maximum Loss = 1431.10 (47.70%)     at price > or = 59.00
Breakeven = 57.57              Current Stock Price = 58.49
-------------------------------------------------------
```

Volatility Can Be Your Friend

"You can't build a reputation on what you are going to do."

Henry Ford

A major factor in stock price movement is market volatility. Books have been written on the subject and specific terminology has been developed to describe various components. I have done a lot of research on it, but it is my experience and observation on what happens during high market volatility that has allowed me to take advantage of it. That is key to your success. Understanding all the terminology and specifics is one thing, but applying the knowledge to making money is the most important. That is what I will try to provide you in this chapter: how you can make Market Volatility your money-making friend.

This chapter is provided after the various types of trades have been presented because I wanted you to learn about options first, and how to formulate good trades. You can be very successful even when market volatility is near normal. The concepts provided here allow you to take advantage of high volatile market conditions that can add to your success.

The terminology used in option volatility is referred to as The Greeks.

Each measure of volatility is named after a different letter in the Greek alphabet and is provided here for basic understanding and discussion.

Delta: The change in the price (premium) of an option relative to the price change of the underlying security.

Gamma: The change in the delta of an option with respect to the change in price of its underlying security.

Theta: The change in the price of an option with respect to a change in its time to expiration.

Vega: The change in the price of an option with respect to its change in volatility.

Zeta: The percentage change in an option's price per one percent change in implied volatility.

Each of these risk measurements contains specific trading information and contributes to an option's premium value. The one to pay the most attention to is delta, since it is the one that is related to the Probability of price Achievement (or Probability of Assignment for options).

Delta is a measure of the price sensitivity of an option at any given moment. It is the expected dollar change in the price of an option for each $1 move in the underlying equity. For example an option with a delta of 50 implies that a $1 change in the underlying equity will result in a $0.50 change in the option. Delta is a dynamic measure whose value will change as the price of the underlying stock, its volatility, and the time until expiration changes. At expiration, delta will approach 100 if an option is in the money, and it will approach zero if it is out of the money. During high volatile period, a delta is your friend since its value is higher.

The two components of an option premium are intrinsic value and time value (extrinsic value). Intrinsic value is defined as the amount by which the strike price of an option is in the money. It is the portion of an option's price that is not lost due to the passage of time. For a call option, intrinsic value is equal to the current price of the underlying asset minus the strike price of the call option. For a put option, intrinsic value is equal to the strike price of the option minus the current price of the underlying asset. If a call or put option were at the money, the intrinsic value would be zero. Likewise, an out-of-the-money call or put option has no intrinsic value. The intrinsic value of an option does not depend on how much time is left until expiration, it simply tells you how much real value you are paying for. If an option has no intrinsic value, then all it really has is time value, which decreases as an option approaches expiration.

Time value (theta) can be defined as the amount by which the price of an option exceeds its intrinsic value. The time value (extrinsic value) of an option is directly related to how much time the option has until expiration. Theta decays over time.

By reviewing option quotes, you will note that an option two months out (until expiration) is worth more than an option that expires in the current month. Theoretically, the option with two months until expiration has a greater chance of ending up in the money than the option expiring this month. The more out-of-the-money an option is, the lower it's cost or value. The probability an extremely out-of-the-money option will increase in value is quite slim. This was discussed and demonstrated in the chapter on Probability of Success.

To take advantage of high volatility let's take a look at what happens during a market correction. The most recent was the one during 2008–09. Here is a chart of the VIX (SP500 volatility index) for the period. The dashed line is drawn to show a normal VIX value. Any time the VIX is above this line it is a period of higher volatility. The potential return from an at-the-money (ATM) call option goes up when the volatility goes up. To confirm this I have taken the DOW 30 stocks and calculated the potential return for at-the-money (ATM) calls during various volatility levels.

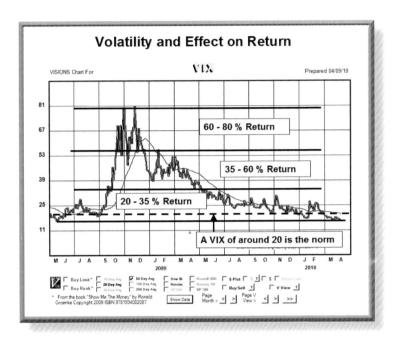

Here is the result for different time periods. The data shows the potential call option return for an at-the-money (ATM) call on all the members of the DOW 30. The holdings are equal-weighted. Note the correlation between the Earnings on Portfolio and the VIX value.

Option Premium Is Also Effected by Market Volatility

I ran the VISIONS Portfolio Income Explorer (PIE) for the DOW 30
on these dates 42 days to expiration.

	09-07-2007	10-10-2008	11-07-2008	06-05-2009
Total Monthly Income	$ 7,739	$ 22,388	$ 15,549	$ 7,714
Total Called Value	$ 400,500	$ 360,700	$ 368,450	$ 341,600
Total Current Value	$ 389,852	$ 345,315	$ 351,786	$ 330,174
Potential Capital Gain	$ 10,648	$ 15,385	$ 16,664	$ 11,426
Potential Yearly Income	$ 92,863	$ 268,650	$ 186,591	$ 104,563
Earnings on Portfolio	23.82 %	77.80 %	53.04 %	31.67%
Days to Expiration	42	42	42	42
VIX Value	26.23	69.95	56.10	29.62

Check Correlation

Option Premium Is Also Effected by Market Volatility

I ran the VISIONS Portfolio Income Explorer (PIE) for the DOW 30
on these dates 42 days to expiration.

	10-09-2009	03-09-2010	10-08-2010	01-07-11
Total Monthly Income	$ 7,736	$ 4,957	$ 5,242	$ 5,556
Total Called Value	$ 364,950	$ 378,700	$ 347,500	$ 396,100
Total Current Value	$ 357,738	$ 369,933	$ 340,708	$ 387,853
Potential Capital Gain	$ 7,212	$ 8,767	$ 6,792	$ 8,247
Potential Yearly Income	$ 92,829	$ 59,486	$ 62,901	$ 66,669
Earnings on Portfolio	25.95 %	16.08 %	18.46 %	17.19 %
Days to Expiration	42	42	42	42
VIX Value	24.18	16.48	20.41	17.40

Check Correlation

Here is the detail for each stock in the Dow 30 on July 8, 2011. The
VIX graph is also provided to demonstrate the correlation. On this

date the VIX was at 16.54 and the return for the first out-of-money call option for the basket was 16.67%.

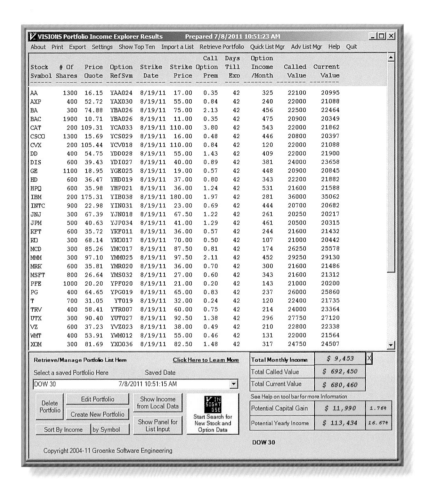

This data is provided with the VISIONS Portfolio Income Explorer (PIE) program.

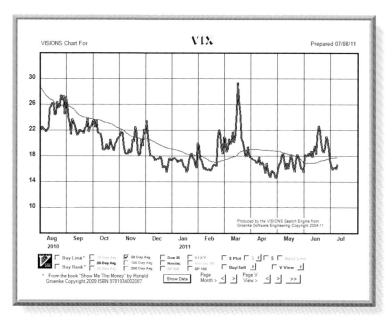

This analysis has shown that during high volatility, option premiums are significantly improved. The Greek factors are available at some brokerage sites. I however look at the VIX as an indication of level of volatility and use P of A to make decisions that will improve my return.

To demonstrate what is possible, here is an example of some option trades that provided excellent returns during a high volatility period. First is the shorthand used to document each trade.

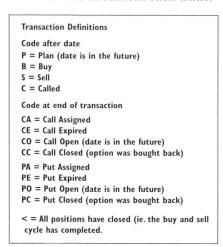

Covered Call and Naked Put Trades During High Market Volatility

```
ULTRA REAL ESTATE                 URE URE JAN APR JUL OCT

04-20-10 S   18 MAY  40.00  1.42   2537.96    2537.96 PA
05-22-10 B      1800  40.00        72010.00  -69472.04
05-21-10 S   18 JUN  40.00  1.85   3311.94  -66160.10 CA
06-18-10 C      1800  40.00        71988.65    5828.55 <
06-21-10 S   18 JUL  42.00  1.90   3401.94    9230.49 PA
07-15-10 B      1600  42.00        67210.00  -57979.51
07-16-10 B       200  42.00         8410.00  -66389.51
07-16-10 S   18 AUG  42.00  1.60   2861.95  -63527.56 CE
08-23-10 S   18 SEP  42.00  1.50   2681.95  -60845.61 CA
09-17-10 C      1800  42.00        75588.59   14742.98 <

             RETURN = $14742/$74400 = 19.81% in 150 DAYS
                                (about 48.21% for a year)


B = Bought, S = Sold, C = Called, P = Plan
CE = Call Expired, CA = Call Assigned, PA = Put Assigned
```

The trades above were based on a strategy of selling out-of-the-money (OTM) 3% or higher return puts and then if assigned, selling a call the next month out. This was repeated during the high volatility period of 2010.

The first trade was a URE May $40 put that was sold on 4-20-11. The P of A (Probability of Assignment) for this option was 7.7%. The return was 3.5% (1.42/40) for 32 days. On 6-18-11, knowing that it would be assigned, (it was in-the-money {ITM} on the day of expiration) a Jun $40 call was sold that produced a 4.5% (1.85/40) return.

That call was assigned, so on the following Monday (6-21-10), another one-month out put (URE July $42 put) was sold for a 4.5% return. The strike was now higher since the stock had moved up. On the Friday of expiration (7-16-10) an Aug $42 call was sold at the same time the put was assigned. That call expired in August and a new one month out Sep $42 call was sold for $1.50 generating a 3.5% return.

That call was assigned at expiration and the opportunity for extra high premiums had passed. The total return for the period was over 19%. On an annualized basis that is around 48%. Looking at the VIX graph below shows that during this period the VIX was in the range of 30 to 45 with a call option potential return of 35% to 60%.

When this type of market condition comes about, it is time to take advantage of the opportunity versus sitting on the sidelines. Being aware of market volatility and by applying the indicators of the VTAM Black Box and Probability of Assignment to your investment decision process, your overall success could be greatly improved. Like the old saying goes, "Make hay while the sun shines."

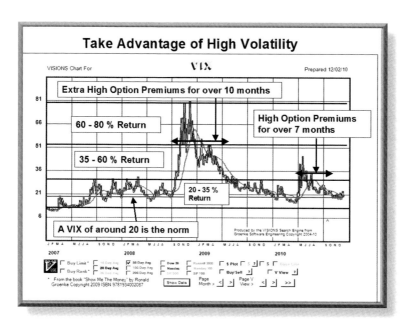

Here is another example from late 2008 when the VIX hit a high of 80 as shown in the VIX chart above. The potential return is in the 60% to 80% range. Actual result was over 9% for an option that was sold on Monday of expiration week. The chances of doing this every week (52 times a year) is very unrealistic. But, if this were repeated each month the return would be over 100%. Trade confirmations have been provided on this trade to show that this is not just made up and all fluff. These are real successful trades that generate an exceptional return in a very short time.

Covered Call Trade During High Market Volatility

```
ULTRA FINANCIAL PRO SHARES    UYG UYG      ALL MONTHS

10-13-08 B     2000  10.13          20270.05  -20270.05
10-13-08 S   20 OCT  10.00  1.15   2279.98  -17990.07 CA
10-20-08 C     2000  10.00         19979.89    1989.82 <

         RETURN = $1989.82/$19979.89 = 9.76% in 7 DAYS

         (even 9.76% for a month = 117.12% for a year)


B = Bought, S = Sold, C = Called, P = Plan
CE = Call Expired, CA = Call Assigned
```

TRADE CONFIRMATION

Account Number:
Account Type:

Account Name:
GROENKE FAMILY TRUST
UAD 02/21/1995

TRADE DATE	SETL DATE	MKT/ CPT	SYMBOL/ CUSIP	BUY/ SELL	QUANTITY	PRICE	ACCT TYPE		
10/13/08	10/16/08	6 1	UYG	BUY	500	$10.1101	Margin	PRINCIPAL	$5,055.05
PROSHARES ULTRA FINANCIALS ETF								COMMISSION	$5.00
								NET AMOUNT	$5,060.05
10/13/08	10/16/08	6 1	UYG	BUY	1,500	$10.14	Margin	PRINCIPAL	$15,210.00
PROSHARES ULTRA FINANCIALS ETF								NET AMOUNT	$15,210.00
10/13/08	10/14/08	5 1	UUFJB	SELL	20	$1.15	Margin	PRINCIPAL	$2,300.00
CALL PROSHARES TR OCT 010 ****								COMMISSION	$20.00
10/18/2008 EXPIRATION DATE								FEE	$0.02
OPEN CONTRACT								NET AMOUNT	$2,279.98

Assignment Confirmation

Transaction History: Transaction Records

Order Type: Sold
Account: Cash for Life - 9499
Trade date: 10/20/2008
Settlement date: 10/22/2008
Security: UYG
Quantity: 2,000
Price: $10.00
Commission & Fees: $19.99
Amount: $19,979.89
Description: PROSHARES ULTRA FINANCIALS ETF OPTION ASSIGNMENT AS OF 10/17/08

This is an excellent strategy that can be very productive. Look for calls or puts with one week or less to expiration. Do at-the-money (ATM) covered calls or slightly out-of-the-money (OTM) puts. Risk may be reduced because of the short time frame. You can take a short-term market view and use the small number of days to expiration in the selection of strike price with a probability of assignment that is in your comfort range. Plan for calls to be assigned and puts to expire. Look at the energy, real estate, gold, or silver sector ETF's for opportunities. The value of these will move around, but a view on where you think they are headed in the short term can add significantly to your yearly return.

Walk the Talk

*"Our prime purpose in this life is to help others. And if
you can't help them, at least don't hurt them."*

Dalai Lama

The following examples are from my trading history folder. They are provided to show how one can generate significant gains in the stock and options market. I will walk you through a number trades that demonstrate the strategies provided earlier.

Double Up

Here is the result of a real trade after Gold started a new up trend in early 2011. GDX is the Gold Miners ETF. When the BUY was signaled on 2-08-11 I initiated a Double Up with an out-of-the-money (OTM) covered call and naked put in a small band to capture some upside in a short-term trade. The call was assigned, and the put expired as planned for a 3.24% gain in 11 days.

```
MARKET VECTOR GOLD MINERS-GDX

02-08-11 B    1000   57.35            57354.60  -57354.60
02-08-11 S  10 FEB   58.00   .72      704.83  -56649.77 CA
02-08-11 S  10 FEB   56.00   .55      534.83  -56114.94 PE
02-18-11 C    1000   58.00           57978.89   1863.95 <

AVG INVESTED       57354.00          GAIN/LOSS     3.24 %

B = Bought, S = Sold, C = Called, P = Plan
PE = Put Expired, CA = Call Assigned
```

Let's walk through the trade detail using the same shorthand as defined in the previous chapter or as found in Appendix B.

On 2-08-11, I bought 1000 shares of GDX at $57.35 for a cost of $57354.60 with commission. That was a debit (-) in the brokerage account. I sold 10 contracts of the GDX Feb $58 call option at $ .72 for a credit of $704.83. The account balance is now negative $56649.77. I then sold 10 Feb $56 puts at $ .55 for a credit of $534.83. The account balance is now negative $56114.94.

On Feb 18 (expiration Friday) my 1000 shares of GDX were called at $58 for a credit of $57978.89. The account balance then was $1863.95 for a gain of 3.24% on the $57354.60 investment.

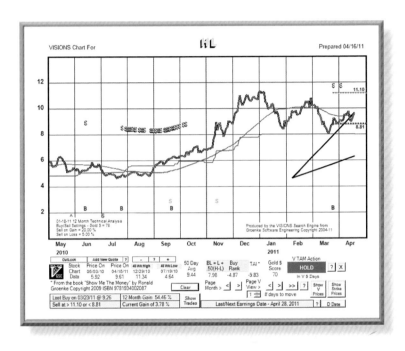

Here are my trades on HL (Hecla Mining) that I identified in the Introduction. Once HL started to trade in the **V** in late February it became a high opportunity and was placed on the potential trade list. Then on March 24, the day after the BUY signal, I initiated an in-the-money (ITM) covered call and an out-of-the-money (OTM) naked put. A new up trend had started, but I wanted to be cautious. The call was assigned and the put expired as planned for a 5.48% gain in less than a month.

```
HELICA MINING—HL

03-24-11 B    10000    9.27         92694.33  -92694.33
03-24-11 S 100 APR     9.00    .63   6218.42  -86475.91 CA
03-24-11 S  50 APR     9.00    .30   1456.74  -85019.17 PE
04-15-11 C    10000    9.00         89956.21    4937.04 <

AVG INVESTED       90000.00        GAIN/LOSS      5.48 %


B = Bought, S = Sold, C = Called, P = Plan
PE = Put Expired, CA = Call Assigned
```

Open Fence

The open fence strategy is one of the higher risk sets of trades that can be undertaken. It requires attention on a daily basis to prevent considerable losses. Success with this strategy requires that you have sufficient knowledge of the underlying equity. That is why it may not be for everyone. I like ETF's in the energy and metals sectors for this type of trade. Oil, natural gas, gold, and silver will always have significant value. They will not go to zero like GM in 2009. The following example demonstrates the concept with very successful trades with the 3x oil ETF ERX. ERX seeks daily investment results, before fees and expenses, of 300% of the price performance of the Russell 1000 Energy Index. The fund invests at least 80% of assets in securities that comprise the index. It will also utilize financial instruments that, in combination, provide leveraged and un-leveraged exposure to the index. The fund is non-diversified.

The graph and trades for ERX are provided below.

The range for ERX in the later part of June 2011 was $62 to $72. Oil was trading in the range of $90 to $96 and the Dow 30 was around 12,000. The market conditions were suggesting that oil should stay in the $90 to $100 range and stock market remain flat or trade slightly up in the next 30 days.

With ERX at $66 on 6-21-11, an Open Fence was established with an $11 addition to the upside and also to the downside. A July $77 strike price was used for selling the call and a $55 strike price was used in selling the put. Only one side of the open fence is at risk at any time. If ERX goes up and approaches the $77 call strike we would buy a position to cover. If the price goes down and is below $55 at expiration we would move the put out and down.

The 6-21-11 trades provided a credit of $3954.55 in the account. ERX made a significant move up at the end of June and at one point on July 1st it approached $76. Realizing that ERX moves at 3x the market, the decision was made to cover before it shot to $77 or higher. 2000 shares of ERX were purchased for $75.86. The July $77 call was purchased back for $2.49 and a new July $75 call was sold at $3.38 to recover the cost and to also establish a point of where ERX may be assigned. This was done to make sure there was some room for ERX to come down before we experienced a significant loss. ERX traded as high as $80.15 on July 7th. On July 14th, one day before expiration, an additional put was sold at a $69 strike price when ERX was trading at $76.25.

On July 15th the $75 call option was assigned and the $55 and $69 puts expired. The return for 25 days was 2.88%.

```
ULTRA ENERGY 3X                  ERX              ALL MONTHS

06-21-11 S   20 JUL   77.00   1.00    1974.80       1974.80 CC
06-21-11 S   20 JUL   55.00   1.00    1979.73       3954.53 PE
07-01-11 B   20 JUL   77.00   2.49    5005.16      -1050.63
07-01-11 B      2000  75.86          151729.00 -152779.63
07-01-11 S   20 JUL   75.00   3.38    6739.66 -146039.97 CA
07-14-11 S   10 JUL   69.00    .30     282.41 -145757.56 PE
07-15-11 C      2000  75.00          149977.13    4219.57 <

AVG INVESTED       146039.97        GAIN/LOSS       2.88 %
```

With ERX trading up and the market down because of the Federal Government Debt crisis, a new ERX open fence was established on July 19. VISIONS Trade Xpress was used to prepare the trade, which is provided below. With ERX trading at $80.76, the upper call strike selected was $95, and the lower put strike selected was $61. These selections are based on probabilities of assignment of less then 1% for the call and 5.14% for the put. If ERX stays in the $95 to $61 range through August 19, a 2.87% return will be generated in 32 days.

```
Open Fence (Short Strangle) for ERX      07/19/11 10:11 AM

Sell 10 ERX Aug 19 2011 95.00 Calls @ 1.10           1084.72
Sell 16 ERX Aug 19 2011 61.00 Puts  @ 1.06           1678.58
Stock Price = 80.76          Breakeven = 58.84 or 92.84
Probability Price > or = 95.00 in 32 Days =      < 1.00 %
Probability Price < or = 61.00 in 32 Days =        5.14 %
Call Value = 95000.00              Put Value = 97600.00
------------------ Open Fence Return -------------------
Call & Put Exp Gain             2763.30    2.87% (32.73 APR)
Call Asgnd & Put Exp Gain       2763.30    2.91% (33.18 APR)
Put Asgnd & Call Exp Gain       2763.30    2.83% (32.29 APR)
-----------------------------------------------------------


TRADES EXECUTED ON 07-19-11

ULTRA ENERGY 3X              ERX              ALL MONTHS

07-19-11 S  10 AUG  95.00  1.10  1082.35      1082.35 CO
07-19-11 S  16 AUG  61.00  1.06  1673.83      2756.18 PO

AVG INVESTED      96300.00        GAIN/LOSS       2.87 %
```

Naked Put

Selling naked puts is a strategy that can provide significant returns. The following example (ERX) uses an oil index ETF that moves in relation to the price of oil and oil service companies. This is a 3x levered ETF that moves three times the market. The naked put being sold is based on a strike price that is less then 80% of the current stock price, very short term, and a P of A (probability of assignment) of less then 5%. This provides a significant return with a low number of assignments. If an assignment takes place, an at-the-money (ATM) call is immediately sold. For the eighteen-month period covered in the example, two assignments took place. The subsequent call for the first put assignment was called as planned. A call for the second put assignment was open when the example was published.

Here is a two-year chart for ERX. Note the long flat periods for the first nine months of 2010, the first 8 months of 2011, and the last 4 months of 2011. These flat periods provide an excellent environment for selling naked puts with low probability of assignment.

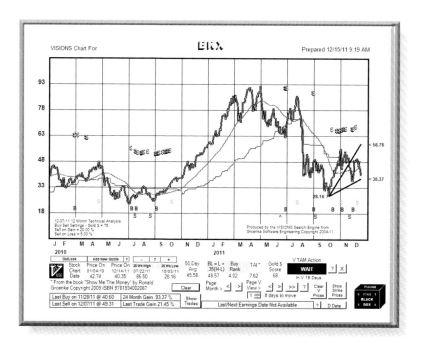

```
ULTRA ENERGY 3X                  ERX ERX      ALL MONTHS

07-22-10 S   20 AUG  24.00   .85   1669.65     1669.65 PE
07-26-10 S   20 AUG  26.00   .92   1819.68     3489.33 PE
07-29-10 S   20 AUG  25.00   .65   1279.69     4769.02 PE
08-04-10 S   20 AUG  28.00   .47    913.70     5682.72 PA
08-12-10 S   20 SEP  24.00  1.15   2274.69     7957.41 PE
08-22-10 B    2000   28.00         56019.99  -48062.58
08-23-10 S   20 SEP  28.00  1.70   3379.67  -44682.91 CA
08-30-10 S   20 SEP  23.00   .60   1174.70  -43508.21 PE
09-03-10 S   20 OCT  24.80  1.10   2179.69  -41328.52 PE
09-08-10 S   20 OCT  23.80   .85   1719.69  -39608.83 PE
09-17-10 S   20 OCT  25.80   .70   1379.69  -38229.14 PE
09-17-10 C    2000   28.00         55979.06   17749.92 <
09-21-10 S   20 OCT  27.80   .70   1379.70   19129.62 PE
09-27-10 S   20 NOV  26.00  1.15   2274.69   21404.31 PE
10-06-10 S   20 NOV  30.00  1.10   2174.69   23579.00 PE
10-11-10 S   20 OCT  34.80   .35    674.71   24253.71 PE
10-13-10 S   20 NOV  32.00  1.00   1979.69   26233.40 PE
11-08-10 S   10 NOV  41.00   .60    584.84   26818.24 PE
11-17-10 S   10 NOV  41.00   .35    334.85   27153.09 PE
11-17-10 S   20 DEC  35.00  1.00   1974.69   29127.78 PE
12-06-10 S   20 JAN  41.80  1.30   2569.65   31697.43 PE
12-10-10 S   20 JAN  43.00  1.10   2179.69   33877.12 PE
12-15-10 S   20 JAN  44.80  1.15   2274.69   36151.81 PE
12-30-10 S   20 JAN  49.80   .65   1279.67   37431.48 PE

01-04-11 S   20 JAN  52.00   .60   1174.68   38606.16 PE
01-12-11 S   20 FEB  54.00  1.55   3074.65   41680.81 PE
01-21-11 S   20 FEB  55.00  1.30   2574.66   44255.47 PE
02-22-11 S   20 MAR  73.00  1.40   2774.65   47030.12 PE
03-04-11 S   10 MAR  74.00  1.10   1082.32   48112.44 PE
03-04-11 S   10 APR  70.00  2.50   2482.30   50594.74 PE
03-07-11 S   10 APR  70.00  2.75   2732.29   53327.03 PE
03-11-11 S   20 APR  64.00  2.62   5214.60   58541.63 PE
03-16-11 S   10 MAR  71.00   .51    492.34   59033.97 PE
03-18-11 S   20 APR  66.00  1.80   3579.62   62613.59 PE
06-06-11 S   10 JUL  70.00  6.40   6382.29   68995.88 PE
06-06-11 S   20 JUL  58.00  2.22   4424.74   73420.62 PE
06-06-11 S   20 JUN  56.00   .51    994.82   74415.44 PE
06-17-11 S   20 JUL  62.00  4.16   8294.68   82710.12 PE
06-21-11 S   20 JUL  55.00  1.00   1979.73   84689.85 PE
06-24-11 S   12 OCT  50.00  4.60   5500.79   90190.64 PA
06-29-11 S   20 JUL  60.00   .75   1474.77   91665.41 PE
09-13-11 S   10 SEP  38.00  1.04   1024.90   92690.31 PE
09-16-11 S   20 OCT  30.00  1.10   2174.72   94865.03 PE
09-27-11 S   20 OCT  26.00  1.02   2014.80   96879.83 PE
10-21-11 B    1200   50.00         60019.99   36859.84
10-21-11 S   12 NOV  50.00  3.96   4304.58   41164.42 CE
11-18-11 S   12 JAN  50.00  6.80   8144.11   49308.53 CO
01-20-12 P    1200   50.00         59980.00  109288.53 <

AVG INVESTED    216000.00        GAIN/LOSS      50.59 %
```

Covered Call

Here is an example of a Gold trade. Gold peaked in late August and then had a correction in September. After about a month, it stabilized at around $1,700 an ounce. After a second Buy signal in late October, I entered a gold position using UGL, which is a 2X gold ETF (moves twice the price of gold). To reduce risk, I executed a covered call that was a little out-of-the-money (OTM) and provided a 5.50% return in 28 days. This allowed me to take a significant gain to the bank without having to wait for gold to move substantially higher. My position was called as planned.

Now everyone immediately asks, "How much money did you leave on the table?" A follow up chart shows that UGL moved up beyond 91, but in early December, it was again below 91. Once it stabilizes, it is a prime candidate for another covered call.

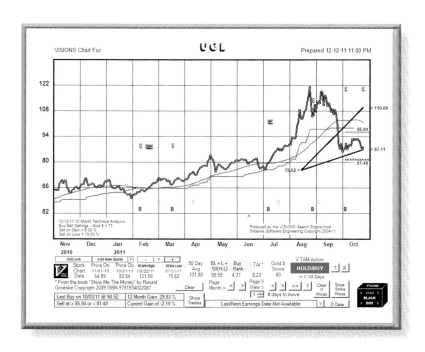

```
2X GOLD BULLION                UGL UGL      ALL MONTHS

10-24-11 B      1000   90.26           90274.20   -90274.20
10-24-11 S    10 NOV   91.00    4.30    4282.33   -85991.87 CA
11-16-11 C       300   91.00           27279.48   -58712.39 <
11-18-11 C       700   91.00           63678.78     4966.39 <

AVG INVESTED          90274.20          GAIN/LOSS      5.50 %
```

Income Portfolios

"Whenever you do a something, act as if all the world were watching."

Thomas Jefferson

"When will interest rates get back to 5%?" Based on the economic situation in 2011, it may take until late 2012 before things start turning around. This is what the VISIONS OutLook Chart shows, which was published in my first book *The Money Tree* in 2002. It is provided again as a guide and a reminder of what to expect in the future. Once things get positive in the economy there could be about 3 or 4 years of expansion and then another significant downturn. Keep this big picture in view as you make your investment decisions.

VISIONS OUTLOOK

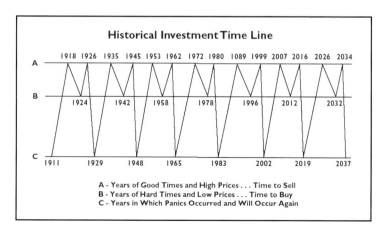

Historical Investment Time Line

A - Years of Good Times and High Prices . . . Time to Sell
B - Years of Hard Times and Low Prices . . . Time to Buy
C - Years in Which Panics Occurred and Will Occur Again

"What is one to do in the meantime?" You can generate income on your portfolio by selling options. Here are two examples. The first portfolio is designed to generate $2000 per month on a $72,000 cash account. If this is done for three years, we have doubled our money ($2000 x 36 = $72,000). No compounding is planned or required. This portfolio uses one ETF in a sector of current importance and generates income by selling deep out-of-the-money puts to protect the downside. If the put is assigned, then a call is sold one month out that again returns $2000 for the month. Once the position is called, a new put is sold and the cycle is repeated. Any additional premium earned is saved for use, if required to maintain the base $72,000 principle.

The trades for a fifteen-month period are provided below. The first table shows each trade as executed and the second table provides a summary by ETF utilized to show how the goal is accomplished.

This portfolio uses mostly 2x and 3x ETF's. These ETF's move two or three times the market. The only time they are owned is when a put gets assigned. The method used for leverage in most leveraged ETF's causes them to lose value faster then their leverage factor, which is disclosed in their prospectus. A call is therefore sold deep enough in the money to force assignment in the next cycle. Look for one month out put options that generate $2000 on an out-of-the-money strike price as deep as possible. Do not worry about leaving money on the table. Discipline is important. All that greed does is get you in trouble. This strategy has had a successful performance for 15 months running. It is easy to implement and provides income of $2000 a month for about two hours of work.

```
SHOW ME THE TRADE MONTHLY INCOME EXAMPLE.

THIS EXAMPLE IS BEING UPDATED OVER TIME TO SHOW WHAT IS POSSIBLE BY USING
THE FEATURES OF THE VISIONS SOFTWARE TO IMPLEMENT THE CONCEPTS IN THE BOOK
SHOW ME THE TRADE by RONALD GROENKE (ISBN # 9781934002223)

THIS EXAMPLE IS FOR LEARNING PURPOSES ONLY. IT IS NOT A RECOMMENDATION.

STRATEGY - EARN $2000 PER MONTH ON A $72,000 CASH ACCOUNT WITH 1X, 2X, AND
           3X ETF'S. UTILIZE VTAM AND P OF A CONCEPTS IN SELLING DEEP OTM
           PUTS FIRST AND THEN IF ASSIGNED, SELL ATM COVERED CALLS TO
           PRESERVE THE INITIAL INVESTMENT. INCOME IS TAKEN OUT EACH MONTH.

INVESTMENT PLAN SUMMARY                                           07-16-11

DATE      TRANSACTION                               (+/- AMOUNT)    BALANCE
--------  ----------------------------------------  ------------   ----------
04-10-10  INITIAL INVESTMENT                        +  72000.00     72000.00
04-20-10  SOLD 18    URE MAY   40.0  PUTS @ 1.4200  +   2537.96     74537.96
04-21-10  CASH WITHDRAWAL                           -   2000.00     72537.96
05-21-10  1800 URE PUT ASSIGNED @ 40.00             -  72010.00       527.96
05-24-10  SOLD 18    URE JUN   40.0  CALLS @ 1.8500 +   3311.94      3839.90
05-24-10  CASH WITHDRAWAL                           -   2000.00      1839.90
06-18-10  1800 URE CALLED @ 40.00                   +  71988.65     73828.55
06-21-10  SOLD 18    URE JUL   42.0  PUTS @ 1.9000  +   3401.94     77230.49
06-21-10  CASH WITHDRAWAL                           -   2000.00     75230.49
07-16-10  1800 URE PUT ASSIGNED @ 42.00             -  75620.00      -389.51
07-19-10  SOLD 18    URE AUG   42.0  CALLS @ 1.6000 +   2861.95      2472.44
07-19-10  CASH WITHDRAWAL                           -   2000.00       472.44
08-23-10  SOLD 18    URE SEP   42.0  CALLS @ 1.5000 +   2681.95      3154.39
08-23-10  CASH WITHDRAWAL                           -   2000.00      1154.39
09-15-10  SOLD 18    URE OCT   42.0  PUTS @ 1.2000  +   2142.46      3296.85
09-17-10  1800 URE CALLED @ 42.00                   +  75588.59     78885.44
09-20-10  CASH WITHDRAWAL                           -   2000.00     76885.44
10-13-10  SOLD 24    ERX NOV   32.0  PUTS @  .9500  +   2257.95     79143.39
10-18-10  CASH WITHDRAWAL                           -   2000.00     77143.39
11-19-10  SOLD 70    UCO DEC   10.0  PUTS @  .4500  +   3092.95     80236.34
11-22-10  CASH WITHDRAWAL                           -   2000.00     78236.34
12-06-10  SOLD 18    ERX JAN   41.8  PUTS @ 1.3000  +   2321.96     80558.30
12-20-10  CASH WITHDRAWAL                           -   2000.00     78558.30

01-21-11  SOLD 16    URE FEB   48.0  PUTS @ 1.3000  +   2063.46     80621.76
01-24-11  CASH WITHDRAWAL                           -   2000.00     78621.76
02-17-11  SOLD 75    UCO MAR   10.0  PUTS @  .3500  +   2561.95     81183.71
02-21-11  CASH WITHDRAWAL                           -   2000.00     79183.71
03-14-11  SOLD 12    UYG APR   62.0  PUTS @ 1.6000  +   1906.10     81089.81
03-21-11  CASH WITHDRAWAL                           -   2000.00     79089.81
04-11-11  SOLD 10    ERX MAY   75.0  PUTS @ 2.3000  +   2287.66     81377.47
04-18-11  CASH WITHDRAWAL                           -   2000.00     79377.47
05-20-11  1000 ERX PUT ASSIGNED @ 75.00             -  75010.00      4367.47
05-20-11  SOLD 10    ERX JUN   73.0  CALLS @ 4.0000 +   3987.62      8355.09
05-23-11  CASH WITHDRAWAL                           -   2000.00      6355.09
06-16-11  SOLD 10    ERX JUL   73.0  CALLS @ 2.0000 +   1987.66      8342.75
06-17-11  CASH WITHDRAWAL                           -   2000.00      6342.75
07-15-11  1000 ERX  CALLED @  73.00                 +  72987.50     79330.25
07-15-11  SOLD 12    ERX AUG   64.0  PUTS @ 1.9500  +   2326.10     81656.35
07-15-11  CASH WITHDRAWAL                           -   2000.00     79656.35

STOCK VALUES AT STRIKE PRICE ON EXPIRATION DATE

INITIAL INVESTMENT              72000.00
STOCK VALUE AT STRIKE PRICE          .0
CASH IN ACCOUNT                 79656.35
CASH WITHWRAWN (YR1 INCOME)     18000.00 (9 MONTHS)
CASH WITHWRAWN (YR2 INCOME)     14000.00

TOTAL PORTFOLIO GAIN            39656.35
                                   55.08 % TOTAL PERIOD
                                    3.67 % PER MONTH
```

117

```
TRADE HISTORY BY ETF

ULTRA REAL ESTATE 2X              URE URE       ALL MONTHS
04-20-10 S  18 MAY  40.00  1.42   2537.91      2537.91 PA
05-21-10 B     1800  40.00       72010.00    -69472.09
05-24-10 S  18 JUN  40.00  1.85   3311.88    -66160.21 CA
06-18-10 C     1800  40.00       71988.65      5828.44 <
06-21-10 S  18 JUL  42.00  1.90   3401.88      9230.32 PA
07-16-10 B     1800  42.00       75620.00    -66389.68
07-19-10 S  18 AUG  42.00  1.60   2861.90    -63527.78 CE
08-23-10 S  18 SEP  42.00  1.50   2681.91    -60845.87 CA
09-15-10 S  18 OCT  42.00  1.20   2141.92    -58703.95 PE
09-17-10 C     1800  42.00       75588.59     16884.64 <
01-21-11 S  16 FEB  48.00  1.30   2063.43     18948.07 PE
AVG INVESTED      75620.00       GAIN/LOSS       25.05 %


ULTRA ENERGY 3X                   ERX ERX       ALL MONTHS
10-13-10 S  24 NOV  32.00   .95   2257.42      2257.42 PE
12-06-10 S  18 JAN  41.80  1.30   2321.92      4579.34 PE
04-11-11 S  10 MAY  75.00  2.30   2287.92      6867.26 PA
05-20-10 B     1000  75.00       75010.00    -68142.74
05-20-11 S  10 JUN  73.00  4.00   3987.86    -64154.88 CE
06-16-11 S  10 JUL  73.00  2.00   1987.93    -62166.95 CE
07-15-10 P     1000  73.00       72987.50     10820.55 <
AVG INVESTED      73000.00       GAIN/LOSS       14.82 %


ULTRA FINANCIAL PRO SHARES 2X UYG UYG    ALL MONTHS
03-14-11 S  12 APR  62.00  1.60   1906.43      1906.43 PE
AVG INVESTED      74400.00       GAIN/LOSS        2.56 %


2X DOW JONES UBS CRUDE OIL     UCO UCO       ALL MONTHS
11-19-10 S  70 DEC  10.00   .45   3092.89      3092.89 PE
02-17-11 S  75 MAR  10.00   .35   2564.16      5657.05 PE
AVG INVESTED      75000.00       GAIN/LOSS        7.54 %
```

The second income portfolio is much more conservative. The goal with this one is to generate $2000 per month on a $200,000 cash account. This is only 1% per month because the strategy is used on an emergency cash reserve. Capital preservation is front and foremost and accomplished by selling deep in-the-money (ITM) calls on two to four ETF's in economic sectors that are not under stress at the time. Trades for six years are provided below. They include the market correction during 2008–09, which demonstrates a stick to the strategy discipline, and a do not panic strategy in the bad times can be very rewarding.

The goal for each year was met except for 2009. A dime was never lost and the portfolio rode through the market correction without difficulty. The $6000 income lost in 2009 was recovered in 2011. This process was successful because the portfolio was always fully invested in equities, and decisions were made to always place asset preservation as the top priority versus higher returns.

I get asked this question a lot. "Why do you show all the details in your trades?" The reason is, I am trying to dispel the myths about options. They are not risky and most investors can be successful by following the principles and using discipline to stay the course. I demonstrate the process and provide a basis for everyone to learn from. This is solid strategy and not a ponzi scheme. You just need to do it to prove to yourself that you too can succeed.

The trades provided next are from the portfolios provided in the VISIONS software. A summary for ScoreCard 3 (1% per month) is provided below.

```
SCORECARD                    3
                          -------
INITIAL INVESTMENT        200000

CALLED VALUE              213335
CASH BALANCE                3457
MARGIN EXPENSE                 0
CASH WITHDRAWEN           154000
                          --------
OVERALL VALUE             370793
          GAIN            170793
             %             85.40

PERIOD (MONTHS)               77
ANNUALIZED GAIN            13.32
```

```
VISIONS STOCK MARKET EXPLORER INVESTMENT EXAMPLE HISTORY        SCORECARD #3

THIS EXAMPLE IS BEING UPDATED OVER TIME TO SHOW WHAT IS POSSIBLE BY USING
THE FEATURES OF THE VISIONS SOFTWARE TO IMPLEMENT THE CONCEPTS IN THE BOOK
SHOW ME THE MONEY by RONALD GROENKE (ISBN # 9781934002087)

THIS EXAMPLE IS FOR LEARNING PURPOSES ONLY. IT IS NOT A RECOMMENDATION.

STRATEGY - EARN 12% A YEAR USING ETF'S. SELL IN-THE-MONEY CALLS PROVIDING
          5-8% DOWNSIDE PROTECTION. SHORT TERM INCOME ACCOUNT.

INVESTMENT PLAN SUMMARY                                        10-25-11

DATE     TRANSACTION                              (+/- AMOUNT)      BALANCE
-------- ---------------------------------------- ------------   -----------
07-01-05 INITIAL INVESTMENT                       +   200000.00   200000.00

07-01-05 BOUGHT 900  SOFTWARE HLDR     @ 35.300   -    31775.00   168225.00
         SOLD  9    SWH NOV 35.00 CALLS @ 1.7500   +     1556.47   169781.47
         CALLED VALUE = 31479.95   SOLD % =  3.97 EXP % =  4.89
07-01-05 BOUGHT 2000 SEMICONDUCTOR HLDR@ 33.80    -    67605.00   102176.47
         SOLD 20    SMH NOV 32.50 CALLS @ 2.8500   +     5664.91   107841.38
         CALLED VALUE = 64978.83   SOLD % =  4.49 EXP % =  8.37
07-01-05 BOUGHT 3000 NASDAQ 100 TRUST  @ 36.730   -   110195.00    -2353.62
         SOLD 30    QQQQ DEC 36.00 CALLS @ 2.4500   +     7299.87     4946.25
         CALLED VALUE =107977.39   SOLD % =  4.61 EXP % =  6.62
07-01-05 CASH WITHDRAWAL                           -     4900.00       46.25
11-18-05 900  SWH  CALLED @  35.00                 +    31479.95    31526.20
11-18-05 2000 SMH  CALLED @  32.50                 +    64978.83    96505.03
11-21-05 BOUGHT 300  OIL SERVICE HLDR  @ 120.040  -    36017.00    60488.03
         SOLD  3    OIH JAN 115.0 CALLS @ 9.3000   +     2774.95    63262.98
         CALLED VALUE = 34479.85   SOLD % =  3.43 EXP % =  7.70
11-21-05 BOUGHT 1000 SOFTWARE HLDR     @ 37.350   -    37355.00    25907.98
         SOLD 10    SWH FEB 37.50 CALLS @ 1.1000   +     1084.98    26992.96
         CALLED VALUE = 37479.75   SOLD % =  3.23 EXP % =  2.90
11-21-05 BOUGHT 700  SEMICONDUCTORHLDR @ 36.480   -    25541.00     1451.96
         SOLD  7    SMH FEB 35.00 CALLS @ 2.5500   +     1769.97     3221.93
         CALLED VALUE = 24480.18   SOLD % =  2.77 EXP % =  6.93
11-21-05 CASH WITHDRAWAL                           -     3000.00      221.93
12-16-05 3000 QQQQ CALLED @  36.00                 +   107977.39   108199.32
12-19-05 BOUGHT 700  NASDAQ 100 TRUST  @ 41.580   -    29111.00    79088.32
         SOLD  7    QQQQ MAR 41.00 CALLS @ 1.8000   +     1244.98    80333.30
         CALLED VALUE = 28680.04   SOLD % =  2.79 EXP % =  4.27
12-19-05 BOUGHT 400  RETAIL HOLDERS TR @ 98.600   -    39445.00    40888.30
         SOLD  4    RTH JAN 100.0 CALLS @ 1.3000   +      504.99    41393.29
         CALLED VALUE = 39979.66   SOLD % =  2.63 EXP % =  1.28
12-19-05 BOUGHT 200  BIOTECH HOLDERS TR@ 200.300  -    40065.00     1328.29
         SOLD  2    BBH APR 185.0 CALLS @22.1000   +     4404.93     5733.22
         CALLED VALUE = 36979.76   SOLD % =  3.29 EXP % = 10.99
12-19-05 CASH WITHDRAWAL                           -     5000.00      733.22

01-20-06 300  OIH  CALLED @ 115.00                 +    34479.85    35213.07
01-23-06 SOLD  4    RTH APR100.00 CALLS @ 1.3000   +      504.98    35718.05
01-23-06 BOUGHT 800  NASDAQ 100 TRUST  @ 41.2800  -    33029.00     2689.05
         SOLD  8    QQQQ JUN 41.00 CALLS @ 2.3000   +     1824.97     4514.02
         CALLED VALUE = 32779.90   SOLD % =  4.77 EXP % =  5.52
01-23-06 CASH WITHDRAWAL                           -     4000.00      514.02
02-17-06 700  SMH  CALLED @  35.00                 +    24480.18    24994.20
02-21-06 SOLD 10    SWH MAY 37.50 CALLS @ 1.5500   +     1534.94    26529.14
02-21-06 BOUGHT 200  OIL SERVICE HLDR  @ 140.380  -    28081.00    -1551.86
         SOLD  2    OIH APR 135.0 CALLS @11.3000   +     2244.96      693.10
         CALLED VALUE = 26980.10   SOLD % =  4.07 EXP % =  7.99
02-21-06 CASH WITHDRAWAL                           -      600.00       93.10
03-20-06 700  QQQQ CALLED @  41.000                +    28680.04    28773.14
03-20-06 BOUGHT 800  SEMICONDUCTORHLDR @ 35.550   -    28445.00      328.14
         SOLD  8    SMH MAY 35.00 CALLS @ 1.8500   +     1464.97     1793.11
         CALLED VALUE = 27980.06   SOLD % =  3.51 EXP % =  5.15
03-20-06 CASH WITHDRAWAL                           -     1700.00       93.11

04-21-06 200  OIH  CALLED @ 135.00                 +    26980.10    27073.21
04-21-06 200  BBH  CALLED @ 185.00                 +    36979.76    64052.97
04-21-06 SOLD  4    RTH JUL 100.0 CALLS @ 1.6000   +      624.97    64677.94
04-21-06 BOUGHT 400  OIL SERVICE HLDR  @ 162.580  -    65037.00     -359.06
         SOLD  4    OIH JUL 150.0 CALLS @19.5000   +     7784.88     7425.82
         CALLED VALUE = 59978.99   SOLD % =  4.19 EXP % = 11.97
04-21-06 CASH WITHDRAWAL                           -     4800.00     2625.82
05-22-06 800  SMH  CALLED @  35.00                 +    27980.06    30605.88
05-22-06 SOLD 10    SWH NOV 37.50 CALLS @  .8500   +      834.97    31440.85
05-22-06 BOUGHT 800  SEMICONDUCTORHLDR @ 34.610   -    27693.00     3747.85
         SOLD  8    SMH AUG 35.00 CALLS @ 1.6500   +     1304.97     5052.82
```

```
04-21-06 200  OIH  CALLED @ 135.00              +    26980.10     27073.21
04-21-06 200  BBH  CALLED @ 185.00              +    36979.76     64052.97
04-21-06 SOLD   4    RTH JUL 100.0 CALLS @ 1.6000  +     624.97     64677.94
04-21-06 BOUGHT 400  OIL SERVICE HLDR  @ 162.580   -   65037.00      -359.06
         SOLD   4    OIH JUL 150.0 CALLS @19.5000   +    7784.88      7425.82
         CALLED VALUE = 59978.99   SOLD % =  4.19 EXP % = 11.97
04-21-06 CASH WITHDRAWAL                         -     4800.00      2625.82
05-22-06 800  SMH  CALLED @  35.00              +    27980.06     30605.88
05-22-06 SOLD 10    SWH NOV 37.50 CALLS @  .8500   +     834.97     31440.85
05-22-06 BOUGHT 800  SEMICONDUCTORHLDR @ 34.610    -   27693.00      3747.85
         SOLD   8    SMH AUG 35.00 CALLS @ 1.6500   +    1304.97      5052.82
         CALLED VALUE = 27980.06   SOLD % =  5.74 EXP % =  4.71
05-22-06 CASH WITHDRAWAL                         -     3000.00      2052.82
06-19-06 SOLD   8    QQQQ AUG 41.00 CALLS @  .3500   +     264.99      2317.81
07-25-06 SOLD   4    OIH OCT 150.0 CALLS @ 5.4000   +    2144.92      4462.73
07-25-06 SOLD   4    RTH OCT 100.0 CALLS @  .7000   +     264.99      4727.72
07-25-06 CASH WITHDRAWAL                         -     3000.00      1727.72
08-21-06 SOLD   8    SMH NOV 35.00 CALLS @ 1.0500   +     824.97      2552.69
08-21-06 SOLD   8    QQQQ DEC 41.00 CALLS @  .8500   +     664.97      3217.66
08-21-06 CASH WITHDRAWAL                         -     2000.00      1217.66
10-23-06 SOLD   4    OIH JAN 150.0 CALLS @ 2.6500   +    1044.96      2262.62
10-23-06 SOLD   4    RTH JAN 100.0 CALLS @ 4.0000   +    1584.94      3847.56
10-23-06 CASH WITHDRAWAL                         -     2000.00      1847.56
11-17-06 1000 SWH  CALLED @  37.50              +    37479.75     39327.31
11-17-06 800  SMH  CALLED @  35.00              +    27980.06     67307.37
11-20-06 BOUGHT 1000 SEMICONDUCTORHLDR @ 35.680    -   35685.00     31622.37
         SOLD 10    SMH JAN 35.00 CALLS @ 1.9500   +    1934.97     33557.34
         CALLED VALUE = 34979.83   SOLD % =  3.44 EXP % =  5.42
11-20-06 CASH WITHDRAWAL                         -     3000.00     30557.34
11-20-06 BOUGHT 900  MKTVECTOR GOLDMNR @ 37.420    -   33683.00     -3125.66
         SOLD   9    GDX JAN 36.00 CALLS @ 3.7000   +    3314.94       189.28
         CALLED VALUE = 32379.92   SOLD % =  5.97 EXP % =  9.84
12-15-06 800  QQQQ CALLED @  41.00              +    32779.90     32969.18
12-18-06 CASH WITHDRAWAL                         -     1000.00     31969.18
12-18-06 BOUGHT 200  OIL SERVICE HLDR  @ 144.940   -   28993.00      2976.18
         SOLD   2    OIH JAN 140.0 CALLS @ 8.4000   +    1664.97      4641.15
         CALLED VALUE = 27980.06   SOLD % =  2.24 EXP % =  5.74

01-19-07 400   RTH  CALLED @ 100.00             +    39979.66     44620.81
01-19-07 900  GDX  CALLED @  36.00              +    32379.92     77000.73
01-22-07 SOLD 10    SMH MAY 35.00 CALLS @ 1.2000   +    1184.96     78185.69
01-22-07 SOLD   6    OIH APR 145.0 CALLS @ 3.8500   +    2294.92     80480.61
01-22-07 CASH WITHDRAWAL                         -     4000.00     76480.61
01-22-07 BOUGHT 400  ISHARES FTSE INDX @ 106.350   -   42545.00     33935.61
         SOLD   4    FXI FEB 102.0 CALLS @ 6.5000   +    2584.96     36520.57
         CALLED VALUE = 40779.64   SOLD % =  1.92 EXP % =  6.07
01-22-07 BOUGHT 1000 MKTVECTOR GOLDMNR @ 37.580    -   37585.00     -1064.43
         SOLD 10    GDX FEB 37.00 CALLS @ 1.5500   +    1534.97       470.54
         CALLED VALUE = 36979.76   SOLD % =  2.47 EXP % =  4.08
02-16-07 400  FXI  CALLED @ 102.00              +    40779.64     41250.18
02-16-07 1000 GDX  CALLED @  37.00              +    36979.76     78229.94
02-20-07 CASH WITHDRAWAL                         -     2000.00     76229.94
02-20-07 BOUGHT 400  ISHARES FTSE INDX @ 107.210   -   42889.00     33340.94
         SOLD   4    FXI MAY 103.0 CALLS @ 8.7000   +    3464.94     36805.88
         CALLED VALUE = 41179.62   SOLD % =  4.09 EXP % =  8.07
02-20-07 BOUGHT 800  NASDAQ 100 TRUST  @ 44.6800   -   35749.00      1056.88
         SOLD   8    QQQQ APR 43.00 CALLS @ 2.7600   +    2192.96      3249.84
         CALLED VALUE = 34379.85   SOLD % =  2.30 EXP % =  6.13
04-20-07 600   OIH  CALLED @ 145.00             +    86978.09     90227.93
04-20-07 800  QQQQ CALLED @  43.00              +    34379.85    124607.78
04-23-07 BOUGHT 400  OIL SERVICE HLDR  @ 151.540   -   60621.00     63986.78
         SOLD   4    OIH JUL 145.0 CALLS @12.1000   +    4824.92     68811.70
         CALLED VALUE = 57979.06   SOLD % =  3.60 EXP % =  7.95
04-23-07 BOUGHT 1600 MKT VECT GOLD MNRS@ 41.4700   -   66357.00      2454.70
         SOLD 16    GDX JUN  40.0 CALLS @ 2.6500   +    4222.93      6677.63
         CALLED VALUE = 63978.86   SOLD % =  2.78 EXP % =  6.36
04-23-07 CASH WITHDRAWAL                         -     4000.00      2677.63
```

```
05-18-07 1000 SMH   CALLED @  35.00                    +    34979.83    37657.46
05-18-07 400  FXI   CALLED @ 103.00                    +    41179.62    78837.08
05-21-07 CASH WITHDRAWAL                                −     2000.00    76837.08
05-21-07 BOUGHT 1700 PSHRS SER/MFG CHK @ 23.3800       −    39742.00    37095.08
         SOLD 17    PGJ SEP  22.0 CALLS @ 2.8000       +     4724.42    41819.50
         CALLED VALUE = 37379.75   SOLD % =  5.94  EXP % = 11.88
05-21-07 BOUGHT 400  ISHRS TEL/FIN CHK @ 114.750       −    45896.00    -4076.50
         SOLD  4    FXI AUG 108.0 CALLS @12.0000       +     4783.92      707.42
         CALLED VALUE = 43179.56   SOLD % =  4.50  EXP % = 10.42
06-18-07 SOLD 16    GDX SEP 40.00 CALLS @ 2.0000       +     3182.89     3890.31
06-18-07 CASH WITHDRAWAL                                −     3000.00      890.31
07-20-07 400  OIH   CALLED @ 145.00                    +    57979.06    58869.37
07-23-07 CASH WITHDRAWAL                                −     5000.00    53869.37
07-23-07 BOUGHT 1500 SEMICONDUCTOR HLDR@ 39.68         −    59525.00    -5655.63
         SOLD 15    SMH NOV 37.50 CALLS @ 3.8500       +     5758.66      103.03
         CALLED VALUE = 56229.12   SOLD % =  4.13  EXP % =  9.67
08-17-07 400  FXI   CALLED @ 108.00                    +    43179.56    43282.59
08-20-07 BOUGHT 1900 SPDR HOMEBUILDERS @ 25.12         −    47733.00    -4450.41
         SOLD 19    XHB SEP 24.00 CALLS @ 2.4500       +     4635.67      185.26
         CALLED VALUE = 45579.48   SOLD % =  5.20  EXP % =  9.71
09-21-07 1700 PGJ   CALLED @  22.00                    +    37379.75    37565.01
09-21-07 1600 GDX   CALLED @  40.00                    +    63978.86   101543.87
09-21-07 SOLD 19    XHB DEC 24.00 CALLS @ 2.0000       +     3780.62   105324.49
09-24-07 CASH WITHDRAWAL                                −     1000.00   104324.49
09-21-07 BOUGHT 1700 US NAT GAS FD ETF @ 38.55         −    65540.00    38784.49
         SOLD 17    UNG JAN 37.00 CALLS @ 5.3000       +     8992.11    47776.60
         CALLED VALUE = 62878.90   SOLD % =  9.66  EXP % = 13.72
09-21-07 BOUGHT 500  ML RETAIL HOLDERS @ 101.9         −    50955.00    -3178.40
         SOLD  5    RTH JAN 100.0 CALLS @ 7.1000       +     3534.94      356.54
         CALLED VALUE = 49979.33   SOLD % =  5.02  EXP % =  6.93
11-20-07 SOLD 15    SMH JAN 35.00 CALLS @  .8500       +     1258.70     1615.24
11-20-07 CASH WITHDRAWAL                                −     1000.00      615.24
12-21-07 SOLD 19    XHB MAR 23.00 CALLS @  .8000       +     1500.70     2115.94
12-21-07 CASH WITHDRAWAL                                −     2000.00      115.94

01-17-08 1700 UNG   CALLED @  37.00                    +    62878.90    62994.84
01-18-08 SOLD 15    SMH MAY 35.00 CALLS @  .2500       +      358.73    63353.57
01-18-08 SOLD  5    RTH APR 100.0 CALLS @  .9500       +      459.98    63813.55
01-18-08 CASH WITHDRAWAL                                −     4000.00    59813.55
01-18-08 BOUGHT 2600 FINANCIAL SEL SPDR@ 25.50         −    66305.00    -6491.45
         SOLD 26    XLF MAR 24.00 CALLS @ 2.5500       +     6605.39      113.94
         CALLED VALUE = 62378.91   SOLD % =  4.04  EXP % =  9.96
03-21-08 2600 XLF   CALLED @  24.00                    +    62378.91    62492.85
03-24-08 SOLD 19    XHB JUN 24.00 CALLS @ 2.1000       +     3970.61    66463.46
03-24-08 CASH WITHDRAWAL                                −     6000.00    60463.46
03-24-08 BOUGHT 800  SPDR HOMEBUILDERS @ 23.48         −    18789.00    41674.46
         SOLD  8    XHB JUN 24.00 CALLS @ 2.1000       +     1664.97    43339.43
         CALLED VALUE = 19180.36   SOLD % = 10.94  EXP % =  8.86
03-24-08 BOUGHT 2000 SPDR TECHNOLOGY    @ 23.10        −    46205.00    -2865.57
         SOLD 20    XLK JUN 22.00 CALLS @ 1.9500       +     3879.94     1014.37
         CALLED VALUE = 43979.53   SOLD % =  3.58  EXP % =  8.39
04-21-08 SOLD  5    RTH JUL 100.0 CALLS @ 3.3000       +     1634.94     2649.31
05-19-08 SOLD 15    SMH AUG 35.00 CALLS @ 1.1900       +     1768.69     4418.00
06-20-08 2000 XLK   CALLED @  22.00                    +    43979.53    48397.53
06-24-08 SOLD 27    XHB SEP 23.00 CALLS @  .4000       +     1064.96    49462.49
06-24-08 BOUGHT 2100 SPDR TECHNOLOGY    @ 23.50        −    49355.00      107.49
         SOLD 21    XLK SEP 23.00 CALLS @ 1.4000       +     2919.20     3026.69
         CALLED VALUE = 48279.39   SOLD % =  3.73  EXP % =  5.91
07-21-08 SOLD  5    RTH OCT 100.0 CALLS @ 1.3500       +      659.97     3686.66
07-21-08 CASH WITHDRAWAL                                −     2000.00     1686.66
08-18-08 SOLD 15    SMH NOV 35.00 CALLS @  .2800       +      403.73     2090.39
08-18-08 CASH WITHDRAWAL                                −     2000.00       90.39
09-22-08 SOLD 27    XHB NOV 23.00 CALLS @ 1.0000       +     2674.66     2765.05
09-22-08 SOLD 21    XLK NOV 23.00 CALLS @  .2000       +      399.23     3164.28
09-22-08 CASH WITHDRAWAL                                −     2000.00     1164.28
10-21-08 SOLD  5    RTH JAN  95.0 CALLS @ 1.0500       +      509.98     1674.26
10-22-08 CASH WITHDRAWAL                                −     1000.00      674.26
```

```
11-24-08 2100 XLK   SOLD @ 14.39                        +    30213.83      30888.09
11-24-08 1500 SMH   SOLD @ 15.78                        +    23664.87      54552.96
11-24-08 2700 XHB   SOLD @ 9.36                         +    25266.86      79819.82
11-24-08 BOUGHT 9200 ULTRA FINANCIALS  @ 4.450          -    40945.00      38874.82
         SOLD 92   UYG MAR 9.000 CALLS @  .7000         +     6365.90      45240.72
         CALLED VALUE = 82778.23   SOLD % =117.70  EXP % = 15.54
11-24-08 BOUGHT 900  ULTRA QQQ        @ 23.65           -    21290.00      23950.72
         SOLD  9   QLD JAN 35.00 CALLS @ 1.1000         +      974.98      24925.70
         CALLED VALUE = 31479.95   SOLD % = 52.40  EXP % =  4.58
11-24-08 BOUGHT 1000 ULTRA SP500      @ 22.55           -    22555.00       2370.70
         SOLD 10   SSO MAR 40.00 CALLS @ 1.4000         +     1384.97       3755.67
         CALLED VALUE = 39979.66   SOLD % = 83.40  EXP % =  6.14
11-24-08 CASH WITHDRAWAL                                -     3000.00        755.67

01-19-09 SOLD  5   RTH APR  95.0 CALLS @  .3000         +      134.99        890.66
01-19-09 SOLD  9   QLD APR  35.0 CALLS @ 1.1000         +      974.96       1865.62
01-19-09 CASH WITHDRAWAL                                -     1000.00        865.62
03-23-09 SOLD 1000 SSO @  20.32                         +    20314.32      21179.94
03-23-09 BOUGHT 8000 ULTRA REAL ESTATE @ 2.480          -    19845.00       1334.94
         SOLD 80   URE JUN 5.000 CALLS @  .1500         +     1134.98       2469.92
         CALLED VALUE = 39979.66   SOLD % =107.20  EXP % =  5.71
03-23-09 SOLD 92   UYG SEP  9.00 CALLS @  .0500         +      385.98       2855.90
03-23-09 CASH WITHDRAWAL                                -     2000.00        855.90
04-20-09 SOLD  5   RTH JUL  90.0 CALLS @ 1.4500         +      709.97       1565.87
04-20-09 SOLD  9   QLD JUL  38.0 CALLS @ 1.7000         +     1514.94       3080.81
04-20-09 CASH WITHDRAWAL                                -     3000.00         80.81
06-19-09 SOLD 80   URE SEP  5.00 CALLS @  .1500         +     1134.96       1215.77
06-19-09 CASH WITHDRAWAL                                -     1000.00        215.77
07-17-09 900  QLD  CALLED @  38.00                      +    34179.86      34395.63
07-20-09 SOLD  5   RTH OCT  85.0 CALLS @ 2.0000         +      984.96      35380.59
07-20-08 BOUGHT 900  ULTRA QQQ        @ 41.20           -    37085.00      -1704.41
         SOLD  9   QLD OCT 42.00 CALLS @ 3.5000         +     3134.95       1430.54
         CALLED VALUE = 37779.74   SOLD % = 10.32  EXP % =  8.45
07-20-09 CASH WITHDRAWAL                                -     1000.00        430.54
09-18-09 8000 URE   CALLED @  5.00                      +    39979.66      40410.20
09-22-09 BOUGHT 6300 ULTRA REAL ESTATE @ 6.320          -    39821.00        589.20
         SOLD 63   URE DEC 7.000 CALLS @  .4000         +     2467.71       3056.91
         CALLED VALUE = 44079.53   SOLD % = 16.89  EXP % =  6.19
09-22-09 SOLD 92   UYG DEC  9.00 CALLS @  .0500         +      385.98       3442.89
09-22-09 CASH WITHDRAWAL                                -     3000.00        442.89
10-16-09 500  RTH  CALLED @  85.00                      +    42479.58      42922.47
10-16-09 900  QLD  CALLED @  42.00                      +    37779.74      80702.21
10-19-09 BOUGHT 2000 SPDR HOMEBUILDERS @ 15.46          -    30925.00      49777.21
         SOLD 20   XHB DEC 15.00 CALLS @ 1.1500         +     2279.96      52057.17
         CALLED VALUE = 29980.00   SOLD % =  4.31  EXP % =  7.37
10-19-09 BOUGHT 1200 UNITED STATES OIL @ 40.30          -    48365.00       3692.17
         SOLD 12   USO NOV 40.00 CALLS @ 2.0000         +     2384.96       6077.13
         CALLED VALUE = 47979.40   SOLD % =  4.13  EXP % =  4.93
10-19-09 CASH WITHDRAWAL                                -     5000.00       1077.13
11-23-09 SOLD 12   USO DEC  40.0 CALLS @ 1.5100         +     1796.94       2874.07
11-23-09 CASH WITHDRAWAL                                -     2000.00        874.07
12-21-09 SOLD 12   USO JAN  40.0 CALLS @  .3400         +      392.98       1267.05
12-21-09 SOLD 63   URE JAN  7.00 CALLS @  .1500         +      892.71       2159.76
12-21-09 SOLD 92   UYG MAR  9.00 CALLS @  .1000         +      845.97       3005.73
12-21-09 SOLD 20   XHB JAN  15.0 CALLS @  .4600         +      899.97       3905.70
12-21-09 CASH WITHDRAWAL                                -     2000.00       1905.70

01-15-10 2000 XHB  CALLED @  15.00                      +    29980.00      31885.70
01-19-10 SOLD 12   USO FEB  40.0 CALLS @  .6000         +      704.97      32590.67
01-19-10 SOLD 63   URE FEB  7.00 CALLS @  .2500         +     1522.69      34113.36
01-19-10 BOUGHT 2000 SPDR FINANCIAL    @ 14.93          -    29865.00       4248.36
         SOLD 20   XLF FEB 15.00 CALLS @  .4000         +      779.98       5028.34
         CALLED VALUE = 29980.00   SOLD % =  2.99  EXP % =  2.61
01-19-10 CASH WITHDRAWAL                                -     4000.00       1028.34
```

```
02-22-10 SOLD 63    URE MAR   7.00 CALLS @  .2000    +    1207.70    2236.04
02-22-10 SOLD 20    XLF MAR  15.0 CALLS @  .1500    +     279.99    2516.03
02-22-10 SOLD 12    USO MAR  40.0 CALLS @  .9500    +    1124.96    3640.99
02-22-10 CASH WITHDRAWAL                            -    3000.00     640.99
03-19-10 6300 URE   CALLED @   7.00               +   44079.53   44720.52
03-19-10 2000 XLF   CALLED @  15.00               +   29980.00   74700.52
03-22-10 SOLD 12    USO APR  40.0 CALLS @  .8700    +    1028.96   75729.48
03-22-10 SOLD 92    UYG JUN   9.00 CALLS @  .0900    +     753.97   76483.45
03-22-10 BOUGHT 5500 ULTRA REAL ESTATE @ 8.080     -   44445.00   32038.45
         SOLD 55    URE JUN 8.000 CALLS @  .7900    +    4298.68   36337.13
         CALLED VALUE = 43979.53   SOLD % =  8.62 EXP % =  9.67
03-22-10 BOUGHT 2000 SPDR HOMEBUILDERS @ 16.39     -   32785.00    3552.13
         SOLD 20    XHB APR 16.00 CALLS @  .7200    +    1419.97    4972.10
         CALLED VALUE = 31979.93   SOLD % =  1.87 EXP % =  4.33
03-22-10 CASH WITHDRAWAL                            -    4000.00     972.10
04-16-10 1200 USO   CALLED @  40.00               +   47979.40   48951.50
04-16-10 2000 XHB   CALLED @  16.00               +   31979.33   80930.83
04-19-10 BOUGHT 2300 ULTRA OIL & GAS    @ 36.43    -   83794.00   -2863.17
         SOLD 23    DIG JUN 36.00 CALLS @ 2.0000    +    4577.67    1714.50
         CALLED VALUE = 82778.23   SOLD % =  4.25 EXP % =  5.46
04-19-10 CASH WITHDRAWAL                            -    1000.00     714.50
06-18-10 1100 URE   CALLED @  40.00               +   43979.53   44694.03
06-23-10 SOLD 20 UYG @ 59.00                       +    1725.00   46419.03
06-23-10 BOUGHT 1200 ULTRA REAL ESTATE @ 39.60     -   47525.00   -1105.97
         SOLD 12    URE JUL 39.00 CALLS @ 2.7000    +    3224.95    2118.98
         CALLED VALUE = 46779.44   SOLD % =  5.21 EXP % =  6.78
06-23-10 SOLD 23    DIG AUG  36.0 CALLS @  .7500    +    1702.69    3821.67
06-23-10 SOLD  9    UYG SEP  80.0 CALLS @  .5200    +     452.98    4274.65
07-16-10 SOLD 12    URE AUG  39.0 CALLS @ 2.5700    +    3068.89    7343.54
07-19-10 CASH WITHDRAWAL                            -    4000.00    3343.54
08-20-10 1200 URE   CALLED @  39.00               +   46779.44   50122.98
08-23-10 BOUGHT 1200 ULTRA REAL ESTATE @ 39.85     -   47825.00    2297.98
         SOLD 12    URE SEP 40.00 CALLS @ 2.3500    +    2804.95    5102.93
         CALLED VALUE = 47979.40   SOLD % =  6.18 EXP % =  5.86
08-20-10 SOLD 23    DIG DEC  36.0 CALLS @  .6500    +    1472.70    6575.63
08-23-10 CASH WITHDRAWAL                            -    2000.00    4575.63
09-17-10 1200 URE   CALLED @  40.00               +   47979.40   52555.03
09-20-10 SOLD  9    UYG DEC  75.0 CALLS @  .5000    +     434.98   52990.01
09-20-10 BOUGHT 1200 ULTRA REAL ESTATE @ 46.55     -   55865.00   -2874.99
         SOLD 12    URE OCT 44.00 CALLS @ 3.5500    +    4244.93    1369.94
         CALLED VALUE = 52779.23   SOLD % =  2.07 EXP % =  7.59
09-20-10 CASH WITHDRAWAL                            -    1000.00     369.94
10-18-10 1200 URE   CALLED @  44.00               +   52779.23   53149.17
10-18-10 BOUGHT 1100 ULTRA REAL ESTATE @ 48.61     -   53476.00    -326.83
         SOLD 11    URE NOV 46.00 CALLS @ 4.2000    +    4604.92    4278.09
         CALLED VALUE = 50579.31   SOLD % =  3.19 EXP % =  8.61
10-18-10 CASH WITHDRAWAL                            -    1000.00    3278.09
11-22-10 SOLD 11    URE DEC  47.0 CALLS @ 1.5000    +    1634.94    4913.03
11-22-10 CASH WITHDRAWAL                            -    2000.00    2913.03

12-17-10 2300 DIG   CALLED @  36.00               +   82778.23   85691.26
12-20-10 SOLD  9    UYG MAR  75.0 CALLS @ 1.3000    +    1154.96   86846.22
12-20-10 SOLD 11    URE JAN  47.0 CALLS @ 1.7200    +    1876.93   88723.15
12-20-10 BOUGHT 1700 DIREXION ENERGY    @ 53.00    -   90105.00   -1381.85
         SOLD 17    ERX JAN 51.00 CALLS @ 4.0000    +    6782.14    5400.29
         CALLED VALUE = 86678.10   SOLD % =  3.72 EXP % =  7.52
12-20-10 CASH WITHDRAWAL                            -    2000.00    3400.29
01-21-11 1100 URE   CALLED @  47.00               +   51679.27   55079.56
01-21-11 1700 ERX   CALLED @  51.00               +   86678.10  141757.66
01-24-11 BOUGHT 1200 DIREXION ENERGY    @ 63.56    -   76277.00   65480.66
         SOLD 17    ERX FEB 58.00 CALLS @ 7.1000    +   12054.81   77535.47
         CALLED VALUE = 69578.67   SOLD % =  7.02 EXP % = 15.80
01-24-11 BOUGHT 1500 ULTRA OIL&GAS      @ 48.79    -   73190.00    4345.47
         SOLD 15    DIG FEB 47.00 CALLS @ 2.9000    +    4333.68    8679.15
         CALLED VALUE = 70478.64   SOLD % =  2.21 EXP % =  5.92
01-24-11 CASH WITHDRAWAL                            -    2000.00    6679.15
```

```
02-18-11 1500 DIG  CALLED @  47.00            +    70478.64     77157.79
02-18-11 1200 ERX  CALLED @  58.00            +    69578.67    146736.46
02-22-11 BOUGHT 1000 MKT VECTORS GOLD  @ 58.43  -   58435.00     88301.46
         SOLD 10   GDX MAR 57.00 CALLS @ 2.4500  +    2434.96     90736.42
         CALLED VALUE = 56979.09   SOLD % =  1.67  EXP % =  4.16
02-22-11 BOUGHT 8500 ULTRA CRUDE OIL   @ 11.50  -   97755.00     -7018.58
         SOLD 85   UCO MAR 10.00 CALLS @ 1.8000  +   15231.01      8212.43
         CALLED VALUE = 84978.16   SOLD % =  2.51  EXP % = 15.58
02-22-11 CASH WITHDRAWAL               -    4000.00      4212.43
03-18-11 8500 UCO  CALLED @  10.00            +    84978.16     89190.59
03-21-11 SOLD 10   GDX APR 57.0 CALLS @ 2.1200  +    2104.93     91295.52
03-21-11 SOLD  9   UYG APR 75.0 CALLS @ .8000   +     704.97     92000.49
03-21-11 BOUGHT 1200 DIREXION ENERGY   @ 81.78  -   98141.00     -6140.51
         SOLD 12   ERX APR 74.00 CALLS @10.0000  +   11984.81      5844.30
         CALLED VALUE = 88778.03   SOLD % =  2.67  EXP % = 12.21
03-21-11 CASH WITHDRAWAL               -    4000.00      1844.30
04-15-11 1000 GDX  CALLED @  57.00            +    56979.09     58823.39
04-15-11 1200 ERX  CALLED @  74.00            +    88778.03    147601.42
04-15-11 SOLD  9   UYG MAY 75.0 CALLS @ .6200   +     542.98    148144.40
04-18-11 BOUGHT 1000 DIREXION ENERGY   @ 76.64  -   76645.00     71499.40
         SOLD 10   ERX MAY 72.00 CALLS @ 6.2900  +    6274.90     77774.30
         CALLED VALUE = 71978.59   SOLD % =  2.09  EXP % =  8.18
04-18-11 BOUGHT 1300 ULTRA REAL ESTATE @ 56.60  -   73585.00      4189.30
         SOLD 13   URE MAY 54.00 CALLS @ 3.7900  +    4911.92      9101.22
         CALLED VALUE = 70178.65   SOLD % =  2.04  EXP % =  6.67
04-18-11 CASH WITHDRAWAL               -    4000.00      5101.22
05-20-11 1000 ERX  CALLED @  72.00            +    71978.59     77079.81
05-20-11 1300 URE  CALLED @  57.00            +    70178.65    147258.46
05-23-11 SOLD  9   UYG JUN 75.0 CALLS @ 1.7600  +    1568.94    148827.40
05-23-11 BOUGHT 1300 ULTRA REAL ESTATE @ 59.50  -   77355.00     71472.40
         SOLD 13   URE JUN 58.00 CALLS @ 3.2000  +    4144.93     75617.33
         CALLED VALUE = 75378.48   SOLD % =  2.80  EXP % =  5.35
05-23-11 BOUGHT 1100 DIREXION ENERGY   @ 69.05  -   75960.00      -342.67
         SOLD 11   ERX JUN 67.00 CALLS @ 4.3500  +    4769.92      4427.25
         CALLED VALUE = 73678.54   SOLD % =  3.27  EXP % =  6.28
05-23-11 CASH WITHDRAWAL               -    4000.00       427.25
06-17-11 SOLD  9   UYG SEP 73.0 CALLS @ .9000   +     794.97      1222.22
06-17-11 SOLD 11   ERX JUL 67.0 CALLS @ 3.9000  +    4274.85      5497.07
06-20-11 SOLD 13   URE JUL 58.0 CALLS @ 2.4600  +    3182.89      8679.96
06-20-11 CASH WITHDRAWAL               -    2000.00      6679.96
07-15-11 1100 ERX  CALLED @  67.00            +    73678.54     80358.50
07-15-11 1300 URE  CALLED @  58.00            +    75378.48    155736.98
07-18-11 BOUGHT 2000 ISHARES SILVER TR @ 39.48  -   78965.00     76771.98
         SOLD 20   SLV AUG 38.00 CALLS @ 2.7700  +    5519.91     82291.89
         CALLED VALUE = 75978.46   SOLD % =  3.20  EXP % =  6.99
07-18-11 BOUGHT 1200 DIREXION ENERGY   @ 76.70  -   92045.00     -9753.11
         SOLD 12   ERX AUG 68.00 CALLS @11.2000  +   13424.79      3671.68
         CALLED VALUE = 81578.27   SOLD % =  3.21  EXP % = 14.58
07-18-11 CASH WITHDRAWAL               -    2000.00      1671.68
08-19-11 2000 SLV  CALLED @  38.00            +    75978.46     77650.14
08-22-11 BOUGHT 2000 ISHARES SILVER TR @ 42.10  -   84205.00     -6554.86
         SOLD 20   SLV SEP 38.00 CALLS @ 5.1500  +   10279.84      3724.98
         CALLED VALUE = 75978.46   SOLD % =  2.43  EXP % = 12.20
08-22-11 SOLD 12   ERX OCT 68.0 CALLS @ .8500   +    1004.96      4729.94
08-22-11 CASH WITHDRAWAL               -    2000.00      2729.94
09-15-11 2000 SLV  CALLED @  38.00            +    75978.46     78708.40
09-19-11 BOUGHT 2000 ISHARES SILVER TR @ 38.83  -   77665.00      1043.40
         SOLD 20   SLV OCT 38.00 CALLS @ 2.2600  +    4499.93      5543.33
         CALLED VALUE = 75978.46   SOLD % =  3.62  EXP % =  5.79
09-19-11 SOLD  9   UYG DEC 62.0 CALLS @ .5600   +     488.98      6032.31
09-19-11 CASH WITHDRAWAL               -    2000.00      4032.31

10-24-11 SOLD 20   SLV NOV 36.0 CALLS @ .2200   +     419.98      4452.29
10-24-11 SOLD 12   ERX NOV 60.0 CALLS @ .8500   +    1004.96      5457.25
10-24-11 CASH WITHDRAWAL               -    2000.00      3457.25
```

```
STOCK VALUES AT STRIKE PRICE ON EXPIRATION DATE

11-18-11 2000 SLV  CALLED @  38.00              +     75978.46     75978.46
11-18-11 1200 ERX  CALLED @  68.00              +     81578.27    157556.73
12-16-11 900  UYG  CALLED @  62.00              +     55779.13    213335.86

INITIAL INVESTMENT                 200000.00
STOCK VALUE AT STRIKE PRICE        213335.86
CASH IN ACCOUNT                      3457.25
CASH WITHWRAWN (YR1 INCOME)         24000.00
CASH WITHWRAWN (YR2 INCOME)         24000.00
CASH WITHWRAWN (YR3 INCOME)         24000.00
CASH WITHWRAWN (YR4 INCOME)         18000.00
CASH WITHWRAWN (YR5 INCOME)         24000.00
CASH WITHWRAWN (YR6 INCOME)         32000.00
CASH WITHWRAWN (YR7 INCOME)          8000.00

TOTAL PORTFOLIO GAIN               170793.11
                                       85.40 %
```

VISIONS Investing Software Tools

"A person with a new idea is a crank until the idea succeeds."

Mark Twain

The VISIONS software created the investing examples and charts provided in this book. VISIONS provide a set of tools that allows you to prepare successful investment plans.

The VISIONS software search engine provides detailed data and filter processes to prepare lists of stocks and options. It gathers the stock and options data from the Internet and presents it in a form that allows decisions to be made on potential return and probability of success.

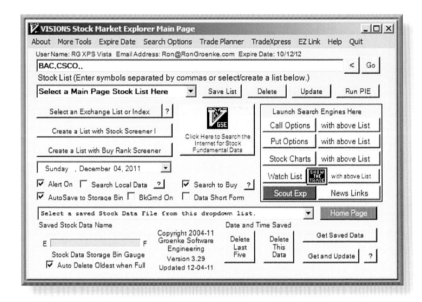

The trade planner allows analysis of various combinations of stock and options that generate the best return. A trade plan feature called TradeXpress implements the algorithms for option selection in conjunction with the Probability of price Achievement. It optimizes the possible return by searching the stock option table data for the best strike price and strike date combinations that generate the highest return in the shortest time possible. You can quickly formulate a set of trades for your investment plan, add your judgment by modifying the selections and perform any number of "What Ifs" as desired. All the examples in the *Show Me the Trade* chapters were provided by TradeXpress.

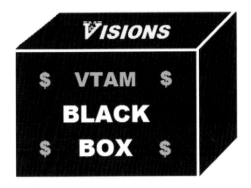

The VISIONS VTAM Black Box provides a trade map and the signals of what to do when on your list of stocks and ETF's. This outstanding program can significantly improve your investing success.

VISIONS Trade Planner

VISIONS Trade Planner

Help Tools Set Fee Schedule Show Symbols Stock Info Show Call Options Show Put Options Start New Plan Save Plan Delete Plan Run PIE Exit

Select a saved Trade Plan from this dropdown box.

Show Me The Trade Example   12-10-11 08:07 AM

For a new plan use this name or Enter your own Plan Name.

Show Me The Trade Example

(Date and Time will be added)

o In N Plan	# of Shares	Type of Trade	Stock Symbol	Stock Price & Quote Date	Option RefSym	Strike Date	Strike Price	S Open Prem & TAI	Days till Exp	Trade Result % Gain If Sold If Exp	Funds to Invest	Naked Put Gain Premium/ Put Margin % Gain or APR
Yes	1000	BuyStk&SellCall	AA	9.64 12/10/11 8:04 AM	FAA025	1/20/12	10.00	0.45	42	OTM 75.76 42.45 8.51 4.77	-9200.12	7.01
Yes	1200	Naked Put	AA	9.64 12/10/11 8:05 AM	FAA024	1/20/12	9.00	0.37	42	OTM 4.11 35.72 P F = 1.17	428.89	2588.89 16.57 or 143.97
Yes	200	BuyStk&SellCall	AXP	48.80 12/10/11 8:05 AM	FAX070	1/20/12	49.00	1.87	42	OTM 37.75 34.10 4.24 3.83	-9406.09	
Yes	300	Naked Put	AXP	48.80 12/10/11 8:05 AM	FAX069	1/20/12	48.00	1.83	42	OTM 3.81 33.11 P F = 0.25	533.86	3413.86 15.64 or 135.90
Yes	600	BuyStk&SellCall	CSCO	18.88 12/10/11 8:05 AM	FCS041	1/20/12	19.00	0.64	42	OTM 35.80 30.18 4.03 3.39	-10964.10	
Yes	600	Naked Put	CSCO	18.88 12/10/11 8:05 AM	FCS040	1/20/12	17.50	0.32	42	OTM 1.83 15.90 P F = 0.58	176.95	2276.95 7.77 or 67.54
Yes	300	BuyStk&SellCall	UCO	42.02 12/10/11 8:05 AM	FUC063	1/20/12	43.00	2.95	42	OTM 18.55 62.50 9.35 7.02	-11741.22	
Yes	300	Naked Put	UCO	42.02 12/10/11 8:05 AM	FUC062	1/20/12	42.00	3.60	42	ATM 8.57 74.48 P F = 0.02	1064.73	3584.73 29.70 or 258.12
Yes	200	BuyStk&SellCall	AGQ	57.79 12/10/11 8:05 AM	FAG041	1/20/12	59.00	5.30	42	OTM 100.24 81.84 11.26 9.17	-10518.27	
Yes	200	Naked Put	AGQ	57.79 12/10/11 8:05 AM	FAG040	1/20/12	57.50	5.80	42	OTM 10.09 87.99 P F = 0.20	1144.71	3444.71 33.23 or 288.79
Yes	200	BuyStk&SellCall	FAS	65.12 12/10/11 8:05 AM	FFA133	1/20/12	66.00	8.15	42	OTM 123.48 111.48 13.87 12.52	-11414.41	
Yes	200	Naked Put	FAS	65.12 12/10/11 8:06 AM	FFA132	1/20/12	65.00	8.85	42	OTM 13.62 110.36 P F = 0.10	1754.56	4354.56 40.29 or 350.16

Net Balance   71859.49
Stock Called Value   68963.08
Trade Plan Gain   10822.57
Stock Put Value   72800.00

Total Put Prem   19663.70
Total Put Prem   5103.70
8.33 %
25.95 %
7.01 %

Calculate Plan
Show Detail for Print
VISIONS TradeXpress

Start Trade Map
CNBC RT Quotes

Copyright 2004-11 Groenke
Software Engineering
Updated 12-05-11
Grace Financial Group

Save Plan
BF for All
Set CC/NP Strike Price Value
Clear All   Exit

VISIONS Trade Plan Detail

```
VISIONS INSIGHT TRADE PLAN SUMMARY                              12-10-11

PLAN TITLE: Show Me The Trade Example                    12-10-11 08:07 AM

DATE     TRANSACTION                              (+/- AMOUNT)     BALANCE
-------- --------------------------------------- -------------  -----------
12-10-11 INITIAL INVESTMENT                       +  130000.00   130000.00

12-10-11 BUY  1000 ALCOA, INC.         @   9.64  -     9645.00   120355.00
         SELL 10  AA    JAN 10.00  CALLS @  0.46  +     444.88   120799.88
         FAA025, OTM, CValue = 9977.60   SOLD % =  8.51  (73.92)
         TAI = GetRdy  42 Days to Exp   EXP  % =  4.77  (41.47)
         Stock Price = 9.64        Prob of Assignment = 57.01 %

12-10-11 SELL 12  AA    JAN 9.00    PUTS @  0.37  +     428.89   121228.77
         FAA024 , OTM, TAI = GetRdy, P F = 1.17   42 Days to Exp
         Cash Required = 10800.00       Return on Cash = 4.11 %
         Stock Price = 9.64        Prob of Assignment = 5.71 %
         PUT MARGIN @ 20 % = 2588.89    GAIN ON MARGIN = 16.57 %

12-10-11 BUY  200  AMERICAN EXPRESS COMP @ 48.80  -     9765.00  111463.77
         SELL 2   AXP   JAN 49.00  CALLS @  1.87  +     358.91   111822.68
         FAX070 , OTM, CValue = 9777.57   SOLD % =  4.24  (36.86)
         TAI = BadIdea  42 Days to Exp  EXP  % =  3.83  (33.30)
         Stock Price = 48.80       Prob of Assignment = 43.11 %

12-10-11 SELL 3   AXP   JAN 48.00   PUTS @  1.83  +     533.86   112356.54
         FAX069 , OTM, TAI = BadIdea, P F = 0.25   42 Days to Exp
         Cash Required = 14400.00       Return on Cash = 3.81 %
         Stock Price = 48.80       Prob of Assignment = 35.75 %
         PUT MARGIN @ 20 % = 3413.86    GAIN ON MARGIN = 15.64 %

12-10-11 BUY  600  CISCO SYSTEMS, INC.   @ 18.88  -    11333.00  101023.54
         SELL 6   CSCO  JAN 19.00  CALLS @  0.64  +     368.90   101392.44
         FCS041 , OTM, CValue = 11377.18 SOLD % =  4.03  (34.98)
         TAI = BadIdea  42 Days to Exp  EXP  % =  3.39  (29.46)
         Stock Price = 18.88       Prob of Assignment = 7.94 %

12-10-11 SELL 6   CSCO  JAN 17.50   PUTS @  0.32  +     176.95   101569.39
         FCS040 , OTM, TAI = BadIdea, P F = 0.58  42 Days to Exp
         Cash Required = 10500.00       Return on Cash = 1.83 %
         Stock Price = 18.88       Prob of Assignment = 13.56 %
         PUT MARGIN @ 20 % = 2276.95    GAIN ON MARGIN = 7.77 %

12-10-11 BUY  300  PROSHARES ULTRA DJ-UB @ 42.02  -    12611.00   88958.39
         SELL 3   UCO   JAN 43.00  CALLS @  2.95  +     869.78    89828.17
         FUC063 , OTM, CValue = 12876.86 SOLD % =  9.35  (81.28)
         TAI = BadIdea  42 Days to Exp  EXP  % =  7.02  (61.01)
         Stock Price = 42.02       Prob of Assignment = 18.55 %

12-10-11 SELL 3   UCO   JAN 39.00   PUTS @  3.60  +    1064.73    90892.90
         FUC062 , OTM, TAI = BadIdea, P F = 1.13   42 Days to Exp
         Cash Required = 11700.00       Return on Cash = 9.23 %
         Stock Price = 40.46       Prob of Assignment = 20.94 %
         PUT MARGIN @ 20 % = 3404.73    GAIN ON MARGIN = 31.27 %

12-10-11 BUY  200  PROSHARES ULTRA SILVE @ 54.11  -    10827.00   80065.90
         SELL 2   AGQ   JAN 59.00  CALLS @  5.30  +    1044.73    81110.63
         FAG041 , OTM, CValue = 11777.30 SOLD % = 18.83 (163.66)
         TAI = GetRdy  42 Days to Exp   EXP  % =  9.79  (85.12)
         Stock Price = 54.11       Prob of Assignment = 69.88 %
```

VISIONS Trade Plan Detail (continued)

```
VISIONS INSIGHT TRADE PLAN SUMMARY                          12-10-11

PLAN TITLE: Show Me The Trade Example              12-10-11 08:07 AM

DATE      TRANSACTION                        (+/- AMOUNT)    BALANCE
--------  ---------------------------------  ------------  ----------
12-10-11 SELL 2   AGQ   JAN 57.50   PUTS @    5.80 +   1144.71   82255.34
         FAGO40 , ITM, TAI = GetRdy, P F = -3.10  42 Days to Exp
         Cash Required = 11500.00        Return on Cash = 10.09 %
         Stock Price = 54.33      Prob of Assignment = 21.15 %
         PUT MARGIN @ 20 % = 3444.71    GAIN ON MARGIN = 33.23 %

12-10-11 BUY  200  DIREXION DAILY FINANC @  61.04  -  12213.00  70042.34
         SELL 2   FAS   JAN 65.00  CALLS @   8.15 +   1614.59   71656.93
         FFA133 , OTM, CValue = 12976.96 SOLD % = 19.84 (172.41)
         TAI = Time2Act  42 Days to Exp  EXP  % = 13.35 (116.03)
         Stock Price = 61.04      Prob of Assignment = 48.36 %

12-10-11 SELL 2   FAS   JAN 64.00   PUTS @   8.85 +   1754.56   73411.49
         FFA132 , ITM, TAI = Time2Act, P F = -2.9 42 Days to Exp
         Cash Required = 12800.00        Return on Cash = 13.83 %
         Stock Price = 61.04      Prob of Assignment = 45.71 %
         PUT MARGIN @ 20 % = 4314.56    GAIN ON MARGIN = 40.67 %

STOCK CALLED ASSIGNMENT VALUES AT STRIKE PRICE ON EXPIRATION DATE

01-20-12 1000    AA    CALLED @ 10.00          +    9977.60    9977.60
01-20-12 200     AXP   CALLED @ 49.00          +    9777.57   19755.17
01-20-12 600     CSCO  CALLED @ 19.00          +   11377.18   31132.35
01-20-12 300     UCO   CALLED @ 43.00          +   12876.86   44009.21
01-20-12 200     AGQ   CALLED @ 59.00          +   11777.30   55786.51
01-20-12 200     FAS   CALLED @ 65.00          +   12976.96   68763.47

STOCK PUT ASSIGNMENT VALUES AT STRIKE PRICE ON EXPIRATION DATE

01-20-12 1200    AA    PUT ASSIGNED @ 9.00     +   10819.99   10819.99
01-20-12 300     AXP   PUT ASSIGNED @ 48.00    +   14419.99   25239.98
01-20-12 600     CSCO  PUT ASSIGNED @ 17.50    +   10519.99   35759.97
01-20-12 300     UCO   PUT ASSIGNED @ 39.00    +   11719.99   47479.96
01-20-12 200     AGQ   PUT ASSIGNED @ 57.50    +   11519.99   58999.95
01-20-12 200     FAS   PUT ASSIGNED @ 64.00    +   12819.99   71819.94

TOTAL NAKED PUT MARGIN              19443.70
TOTAL NAKED PUT PREMIUM              5103.70
NAKED PUT GAIN ON MARGIN             26.25 %

INITIAL INVESTMENT                 130000.00
STOCK CALLED VALUE AT STRIKE PRICE  68763.47
CASH IN ACCOUNT                     73411.49

TOTAL PORTFOLIO GAIN                12174.96
                                     9.37 %
```

VISIONS TradeXpress

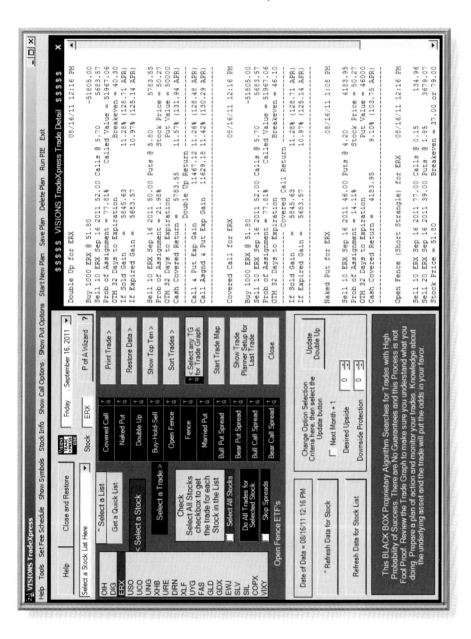

133

VISIONS VTAM Black Box

The VISIONS VTAM Black Box implements the algorithm that provides the chart settings for the BUY-HOLD-SELL signal for any stock or ETF. It is an automated process that continuously optimizes the return for any stock or ETF.

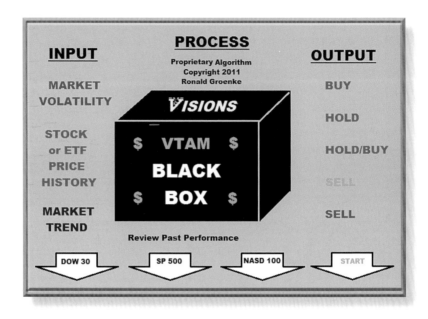

VISIONS VTAM Black Box Processing

The following form shows the Black Box processing in action. The current best return is displayed as the search for the optimum VTAM settings are performed.

135

VISIONS VTAM Black Box Trade Map

The following form shows a Trade Map for a list of stocks and ETF's that are being considered. A detail chart for AXP is being reviewed.

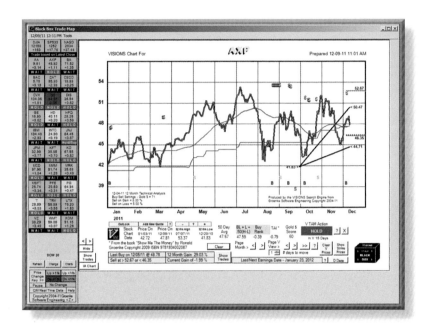

VISIONS VTAM Black Box Trade History

The following form shows the detailed trades for the stock selected.

```
VISIONS Chart Buy/Sell Trade Report for AXP on 12/13/11

Buy Limit Fraction = 0.50 and High/Low Range = 52 weeks.

Buy when number of up days = 3, trading in the Groenke V for 20 days,
currently trading in the V or within +/- 5.0 % of the 50 day average,
and with a VISIONS Chart Gold $ Score that is >= 71.

Sell on upside gain of 8.0 % (after a downturn) or when loss > 5.0 %

These criteria if followed provided a 12 Month Gain of 29.19 %

Buy   on 01/04/11 @ 43.26
Sell on 05/04/11 @ 49.32 for gain of 6.06/Share or 14.01 %

Buy   on 08/22/11 @ 44.42
Sell on 09/01/11 @ 49.29 for gain of 4.87/Share or 10.96 %

Buy   on 09/14/11 @ 48.79
Sell on 09/23/11 @ 46.26 for gain of -2.53/Share or -5.19 %

Buy   on 10/06/11 @ 44.43
Sell on 10/25/11 @ 49.42 for gain of 4.99/Share or 11.23 %

Buy   on 12/05/11 @ 48.78
Waiting to Sell        Current Gain of -1.82 %
```

Download Free Trial Software

at

www.RonGroenke.com

Glossary

American Stock Exchange (AMEX)—a private, not-for-profit corporation, located in New York City that handles approximately one-fifth of all securities trades within the United States.

American Style Option—an option contract that can be exercised at any time between the date of purchase and the expiration date. The other type of contract is the European Style, which may be exercised only during a specified period of time just prior to its expiration. Most exchange-traded options are American style.

Arbitrage—the simultaneous purchase and sale of identical financial instruments in order to make a profit where the selling price is higher than the buying price.

Arbitrageur—an individual that takes advantage of momentary disparities in prices between markets, which enables one to lock in profits because the selling price is higher than the buying price.

Ask Price—the current cost to buy a security or option. It's the lowest price the seller will accept at that time.

At-The-Money (ATM)—when an option's strike price is the same as the price of the underlying stock.

Automatic Exercise—the automatic exercise of an option that is in the money on expiration date.

Bare Cash—a company's cash plus marketable securities less long-term debt.

Bear—an investor whose sentiment or belief is that a security or the market is falling or is expected to fall.

Bear Call Spread—a strategy in which a trader sells a lower strike call and buys a higher strike call to create a trade with limited profit and limited risk. A fall in the price of the underlying stock increases the value of the spread. This is a net credit (cash inflow) transaction. The maximum loss is the difference between the strike prices less the credit. The maximum gain equals the credit.

Bear Market—the stock market cycle where prices for the overall market fall for an extended period of time, usually caused by a weak economy and subsequent decreased corporate profits. It is generally agreed that a bear market is when the stock market experiences a price decline of twenty percent or more, and lasts at least two months.

Bear Put Spread—a strategy in which a trader sells a lower strike put and buys a higher strike put to create a trade with limited profit and limited risk. A fall in the price of the underlying stock increases the value of the spread. This is a net debit (cash outflow) transaction. The maximum gain is the difference between the strike prices less the debit. The maximum loss is equal to the debit.

Bid Price—the current price you would receive if a stock (or option) were sold. It is the highest price the buyer will pay for that security at the present time.

Black Box—A computerized trading system that provides trading instructions based on secret algorithms and models.

Black Scholes Formula—a pricing model that is used by most options exchanges to price various options. It factors in the current stock price, strike price, time until expiration, current interest rates, and volatility of the underlying security.

Break-even—the price of an underlying security at which an option strategy neither gains nor loses money.

Bull—an investor whose sentiment or belief is that a security or the market is rising or is expected to rise.

Bull Market—the stock market cycle where prices for the overall market rise for an extended period of time, usually caused by a strong economy and subsequent increased corporate profits.

Bull Call Spread—a strategy in which a trader buys a lower strike call and sells a higher strike call to create a trade with limited profit and limited risk. A rise in the price of the underlying stock increases the value of the spread. This is a net debit (cash outflow) transaction. The maximum loss is equal to the initial debit. The maximum gain is the difference between the strike prices less the debit.

Bull Put Spread—a strategy in which a trader sells a higher strike put and buys a lower strike put to create a trade with limited profit and limited risk. A rise in the price of the underlying stock increases the value of the spread. This is a net credit (cash inflow) transaction. The maximum loss is the difference between the strike prices less credit. The maximum gain is equal to the credit.

Buy Limit—the maximum price that should ever be paid for a stock, based on its 52 week low (L) and 52 week high (H).

$$\text{Buy Limit} = L + .25 \times (H - L)$$

Buy Rank—a formula to rank the relative appeal of stocks on the prospect list.

In the formula BL is Buy Limit, CP is current price, H is the 52-week high and L is the 52-week low.

$$\text{Buy Rank} = \frac{10 \times (BL - CP)}{.25 \times (H - L)}$$

Call Option—a contract that gives the holder the right (but not the obligation) to buy a specific stock at a predetermined price on or before a certain date (called the expiration date).

Chicago Board Options Exchange (CBOE)—the largest options exchange in the United States.

Covered Call—a short call option position against a long position in the underlying stock or index.

Covered Put—a short put option position against a short position in the underlying stock or index.

Delta—change in the price (premium) of an option relative to the price change of the underlying security.

Double Up—a strategy where one executes both a covered call and naked put with the same expiration date.

Earnings—A company's revenues minus cost of sales, operating expenses, and taxes, over a given period of time.

European Style Option—an option contract that may be exercised only during a specified period of time just prior to its expiration.

Exercise—implementing an option owner's right to buy or sell the underlying security.

Exercise Price—see strike price.

Expiration—the date and time after which an option may no longer be exercised.

Expiration Date—the last day on which an option may be exercised.

Fence—a strategy in which a trader has a long position in a stock or index and buys a put for downside protection which is financed with the selling of a call.

Fundamental Analysis—evaluating a company to determine if it is a good investment risk. Evaluation is based mainly on balance sheet and income statements, past records of earnings, sales, assets, management, products and services.

Gamma—change in the delta of an option with respect to the change in price of its underlying security.

Go Long—to buy securities or options.

Gold $—chart calculation that indicates when to take action and invest in the stock being watched. It is 10 x number of up days, plus 2 x number of days in the VISIONS View V, plus 30, if currently trading in the V, or within 5% of the 50 day moving average. A value of 100 is ideal.

Good 'Till Canceled Order (GTC)—Sometimes simply called GTC, it means an order to buy or sell stock that is good until you cancel it.

Go Short—to sell securities or options.

Holder—one who purchases an option.

Index—an index is a group of stocks, which can be traded as one portfolio, such as the S&P 500. Broad-based indexes cover a wide range of industries and companies and narrow-based indexes cover stocks in one industry or economic sector.

Index Options—call and put options on indexes of stocks that allow investors to trade in a specific industry group or market without having to buy all the stocks individually.

In the Money (ITM)—an option is In the Money to the extent it has intrinsic value. A call option is said to be In the Money when the price of the underlying stock is higher than the strike price of the option. A put option is said to be In the Money when the price of the underlying stock is lower than the strike price of the option.

Intrinsic Value—a call option premium is said to have intrinsic value to the extent the stock price exceeds the strike price. A put option premium is said to have intrinsic value to the extent the strike price exceeds the stock price. The total value of the premium is intrinsic value (if any) plus the time value.

Investor—a person who commits money in order to earn a financial return.

LEAPS (Long-term Equity AnticiPation Securities)—long dated options with expiration dates up to three years in the future.

Limit Order—a condition on a transaction to buy at or below a specified price or to sell at or above a specified price.

Long—a long position indicates that a stock, index, or option is owned.

Margin—a loan by a broker to allow an investor to buy more stocks or options than available money (cash) in the account.

Margin Requirements (Options)—the amount of cash an uncovered (naked) option writer is required to deposit and maintain to cover his daily position price changes.

Market Cap—a company's market capitalization, which equals the number of outstanding shares times the current market price.

Market Order—an order that is filled immediately upon reaching the trading floor at the next best available price.

Married Put—a strategy in which a trader has a long position in a stock or index and buys a put for downside protection.

Naked Call—a short call option in which the writer does not own the underlying security. It is the same as Uncovered Call.

Naked Put—a short put option in which the writer does not have a corresponding short position on the underlying security. It is the same as Uncovered Put.

NASDAQ National Association of Securities Dealers Automated Quotations—a computerized system providing brokers and dealers with price quotations for securities traded over the counter as well as for many New York Stock Exchange listed securities.

New York Stock Exchange (NYSE)—the largest stock exchange in the United States.

Open Fence—a position consisting of a short call and a short put, where both options have the same underlying security, the same expiration date, but different strike prices. This is also sometimes referred to as a short strangle.

Option—a security that represents the right, but not the obligation, to buy or sell a specified amount of an underlying security (stock, bond, futures contract, etc.) at a specified price within a specified time.

Option Class—a group of calls or a group of puts on the same stock.

Option Holder—the buyer of either a call or put option.

Option Premium—the price it paid to buy an option or the price received for selling an option.

Option Series—call or put options in the same class that have the same expiration date and strike price.

Option Writer—the seller of either a call or put option.

Out-of-the-Money—an option whose exercise price has no intrinsic value.

Out-of-the-Money Option (OTM)—a call option is Out of the Money if its exercise or strike price is above the current market price of the underlying security. A put option is Out of the Money if its exercise price is below the current market price of the underlying security.

Portfolio Income Explorer—software program that searches for the best call options for any list of stocks at any time.

Premium—see Option Premium.

Price to Earnings Ratio (PE)—the current stock price divided by the earnings per share for the past year.

Probability—a mathematical basis for prediction that for an exhaustive set of outcomes is the ratio of the outcomes that would produce a given event to the total number of possible outcomes.

P of A—See Probability of price Achievement.

Probability of price Achievement—a mathematical basis for determining the probability that a stock may achieve a specific price in a specific time frame.

Put Factor—a formula to guide the selection of a naked put strike price and strike month. A factor greater than one is desirable. In the formula, PR is the naked put premium, SP is the strike price, CP is the current stock price, and ME is months to expiration.

$$\text{Put Factor} = \frac{6}{ME} \times \frac{100 \text{ PR}}{SP} \times \frac{CP - SP}{SP}$$

Put Option—a contract that gives the right (but not the obligation) to sell a specific stock at a predetermined price on or before a certain date (called the expiration date).

Revenue—amount of money a company brought in during the time period covered by the income statement. This is usually the first line on any income statement and is also sometimes referred to as total sales.

Ride the Wave—a strategy where one sells covered calls and naked puts on the same stock over and over as the stock trades in a wave-like pattern.

Sales—amount of money a company brought in during the time period covered by the income statement. This is usually the first line on any income statement and is also sometimes referred to as total revenue.

Security—a trading instrument such as stocks, bonds, and short-term investments.

Short—a short position indicates that a stock, index, or option is not owned.

Spread—the price gap between the bid and ask price of a stock.

Stock—a share of a company's stock translates into ownership of part of the company.

Stock Split—an increase in the number of stock shares with a corresponding decrease in the par value of a company's stock.

Straddle—a position consisting of a long call and a long put, or a short call and a short put, where both options have the same underlying security, strike price and expiration date.

Strangle—a position consisting of a long call and a long put or a short call and a short put, where both options have the same underlying security, the same expiration date, but different strike prices.

Strike Price—also called the exercise price, it is the price at which a call option holder can purchase the underlying stock by exercising the option, and is the price at which a put option holder can sell the underlying stock by exercising the option.

Technical Analysis—a method of evaluating securities and options by analyzing statistics generated by market activity, such as past high/low, up/down volume, momentum and moving averages.

Theta—change in the price of an option with respect to a change in its time to expiration.

Time Value—an option's premium consists of two parts: time value and intrinsic value. (See Intrinsic Value) The time value portion of the premium deteriorates with the passage of time and becomes zero with the expiration of the option.

Trade—To buy and sell regularly.

Trader—A person whose business is buying and selling.

Triple Witching Day—the third Friday in March, June, September and December when U.S. options, future options, and index options all expire on the same day.

Uncovered Call—a short call option in which the writer does not own the underlying security.

Uncovered Put—a short put option in which the writer does not have a corresponding short position on the underlying security.

Vega—Change in the price of an option with respect to its change in volatility.

VISIONS Portfolio Income Explorer—a Personal Internet Search Engine that can find the best call options for any list of stocks. It returns the best near term call option and calculates the potential monthly and yearly income.

VISIONS Stock Explorer—a Personal Internet Search Engine that gets the fundamental data on any stock and provides all the technical indicators on a VISIONS stock chart.

VISIONS Stock Market Explorer—a full featured Personal Internet Search Engine that can find the best stocks and call or put options that meet various search criteria. It provides tools for information filtering and sorting. It provides stock charts, which include the Buy Limit, 50-Day Average, Buy Rank, the VISIONS View V, and take action indicators.

VISIONS View V—an indicator on a VISIONS chart that shows when it is time to take action and invest in a particular stock.

Web Site—An information location on the Internet. Each web site has a unique address called a URL that one uses to access the site and obtain information or transact business. The URL to download the VISIONS software is www .RonGroenke.com. The URL for Keller Publishing is www.KellerPublishing .com.

Writer—the seller of an option.

Zeta—The percentage change in an option's price per one percent change in implied volatility.

Probability of Assignment
for Call and Put Options

P of A for Call Options

The P of A concept is applied in the use of call options to determine the probability of whether a call option will be assigned or not. The Call Assignment probability calculation is the same as that for the probability of price achievement. Below is the terminology applied when considering the use of call options.

PCA = Probability of Call Assignment

PCA1 = (Tdays-Days2Exp)/Tdays x Adays/Days2Exp

PCA2 = Days2Exp/Tdays x Bdays/(Tdays-Days2Exp)

PCA = 100 *(PCA1 + PCA2)

Where:

Days2Exp = Number of days to expiration based on the date of the option quote.

Tdays = 252 for Days2Exp <= 252

Tdays = 504 for Days2Exp > 252 and <= 504

Tdays = 756 for Days2Exp > 504

Adays = Number of days the stock price was above the strike price in the last Days2Exp days.

Bdays = Number of days the stock price was above the strike price in the last Tdays up and until the last Days2Exp days.

The concept here is the stock price is likely to follow the pattern of the last number of trading days equal to the number of days to expiration. The number of times the stock price has traded above the chosen strike price is weighted by the number of days until expiration versus the total number of days being considered.

The longer the period to expiration, the higher the probability of assignment will occur.

A probability of less than .01 (1%) is possible when a stock has not traded above the strike price for the period under consideration.

Assignments are always possible on good news and analyst upgrades.

The probability table is now tailored to specific prices (strike prices) and dates (expiration dates).

P of A for Put Options

The P of A concept is applied in the use of put options to determine the probability a put option will be assigned or not. This is very handy in selecting put strike prices that improve the probability a naked put will not be assigned.

The calculation for the Put Assignment probability is as follows:

PPA = Probability of Put Assignment

PPA1 = (Tdays-Days2Exp)/Tdays x Adays/Days2Exp

PPA2 = Days2Exp/Tdays x Bdays/(Tdays-Days2Exp)

PPA = 100 *(PPA1 + PPA2)

Where:

Days2Exp = Number of days to expiration based on the date of the option quote.

Tdays = 252 for Days2Exp <= 252

Tdays = 504 for Days2Exp > 252 and <= 504

Tdays = 756 for Days2Exp > 504

Adays = Number of days the stock price was below the strike price in the last Days2Exp days.

Bdays = Number of days the stock price was below the strike price in the last Tdays up and until the last Days2Exp days.

The concept here is the stock price is likely to follow the pattern of the last number of trading days equal to the number of days to expiration. The number of times the stock price has traded below the chosen strike price is weighted by the number of days until expiration versus the total number of days being considered.

The amount of time to expiration increases the probability of assignment will occur.

A probability of less than .01 (1%) is possible when a stock has not traded below the strike price for the period under consideration.

Caution is issued since a stock can drop significantly due to unfavorable news or international events like war and terrorism. Assignments are therefore always possible.

How about a crystal ball for determining future stock prices or direction? How about another opportunity to get an advantage when making investment decisions? This possibility is available with a technique called OutLook. We take the P of A process one step further and project the price of any stock or ETF out fifty days in time. The process looks at the price movement the last 50 trading days and projects the stock motion forward with a Monte Carlo simulation technique. You select the trend for the outlook based on the current stock direction or trends of major indexes.

Here is an example with American Express (AXP). An outlook was created on 4-15-2011. It indicated that AXP should be in the 46–47 range fifty days out. The actual result was around 48, which shows that OutLook did a great job of showing what might happen. This view can help in your selection of option strike date and strike price, thus increasing the number of successful trades.

OutLook is available on any VISIONS chart.

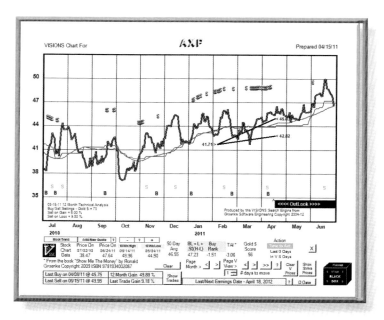

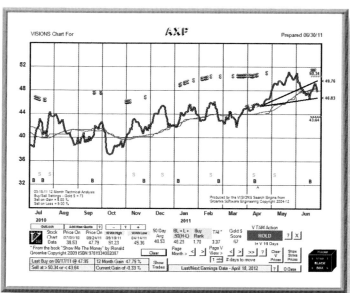

Placing the Trade

When placing option trading orders it is very important to state exactly what is intended. If a mistake is made and you execute a wrong trade you may incur a loss to undo it.

Option orders, like stock orders, can be placed in your brokerage account over the phone by calling a trader, or over the Internet with online access to your account. No matter which way you trade, the way an order is placed is important.

Here are some key terms you should know.

Sell to Open—You are opening a short position for a specific option. This is what you use to write a covered call.

Buy to Close—You are buying back an option you previously sold, to close out the option. This is what you would do if you did not want your stock to be called. Also, you would want to do this if you want to sell the stock. Selling the stock without buying back the call option would leave you in a high-risk, uncovered position.

Buy to Open—You are opening a long position for a specific option. This is what you do when you are taking a leveraged position by buying the option instead of the stock.

Sell to Close—You are closing a long position for a specific option. This is what you do to capture a gain on your leveraged position.

Market order—The order will be executed at the next available bid price. Use this to buy or sell immediately.

Limit order—The order is executed at the limit price or even better if possible.

For the day—The order called a Day order will expire at the end of the trading day.

All or none (AON)—Buy or sell the number of contracts specified. This condition is used to reduce the possibility of trading only one or a small number of contracts in a multiple contract order. Additional orders may increase your overall commission cost.

Good till canceled (GTC)—The order is open until it is canceled. Most brokerage firms will close GTC orders after ninety days.

Trade Data Nomenclature

Transaction Definitions

Code after date

P = Plan (date is in the future)
B = Buy
S = Sell
C = Called

Code at end of transaction

CA = Call Assigned
CE = Call Expired
CO = Call Open (date is in the future)
CC = Call Closed (option was bought back)

PA = Put Assigned
PE = Put Expired
PO = Put Open (date is in the future)
PC = Put Closed (option was bought back)

< = All positions have closed (ie. the buy and sell cycle has completed).

Investor Comments

The first Ronald Groenke book I read was *Covered Calls and Naked Puts* followed by *Cash for Life* and *Show Me The Money*. I also attended his seminar in November 2007.

I use VISIONS Software and follow the trading methodology outlined in his books to pick my trading candidates. I have been trading for 16 years and started to use Ron's system and software after I read his first book and found it to be the most effective method of trading to be able to maximize profits and limit losses. I would like to thank you for all the help your books have given me in continuing as a successful trader!

Bob Anderson
Murray, Utah

I have read all of Ron's books and have attended several of his seminars. As a 78 year old investor, I have participated in several other programs. However, none have been as informative and easy to understand and use as Ron's program called VISIONS. Finally, I find the entire program of books and seminars just plain fun.

Dale Anderson
Muncy, PA

I have been successfully trading stock options for close to two years now. I decided to get into options trading after reading Ron's book *Show Me the Money* and learning about his Vision tool. The vast majority of my best trades during the last two years have come from using Ron's Vision tool. Even when I look at other tools that analyze the market, I still use Vision to help me make my final decision. Ron's method for selecting the best covered call and naked put opportunities leaves me comfortable with my stock option selections.

Brent Artrip
Wake Forest, NC

The seminar was very helpful especially in using to learn to use the trade planner at options expiration each month. I have been able to retire using covered calls and naked puts as a source of income which has much exceeded the usual 4% figure bantered about as the maximum to withdraw from a retirement account. We have also grown the account using Ron's methods. All five of my accounts have beaten the S&P 500, Dow and Nasdaq Composit Indexes.

Dr. David Bankston
Overland Park, Kansas

Ron Groenke has created by far one of the best covered call methods around. I have followed his methodology for over 4 years and IT WORKS! Any type of investing requires discipline and a rational approach. If you have the discipline this book will provide the rational approach and it could also work for you.

I then went on to try the VISIONS software; I paper traded for two weeks and then I purchased it. I didn't even wait for the trial subscriptions to run out. When I started using VISIONS everything changed. VISIONS is easy to use and packed with more functionality and in-line help than software costing a whole lot more. I run VISIONS every evening; review the output and set up my trades for the next day. I place my trades late morning and check later in the day to see my results. In the four years that I've used VISIONS I have financed my first son's entire college tuition using Ron's program. I am now financing my second son's college tuition as well, he has two years to go. I would strongly recommend reading Ron's books and giving VISONS a test drive.

Charles Cirronella
Rockville Centre, NY

Ron is the real deal and his stock and options trading sytem is the best I have found.

John Bowden
Indio, CA

Ron's books have helped me consistently make double digit returns since I started investing like he teaches in his books. I have studied hundreds of hours and have found that most people sell hype and how they got lucky one time. Ron shows his actual trades and a consistent way to get great returns year after year. Thanks Ron!

Mike Braunschmidt
Highlands Ranch, CO

I was talking to my retired financial planner one day about the market, and how to make it more profitable. He told me about covered calls, and explained how they work. He then told me about a book called *Show Me the Money* by Ron Groenke. He called Keller Publishing and had them send me a copy. I read it in just a few hours, so easy to understand and follow. I started doing covered calls right away, with great results. Where else could you get approximately 3% per month income from your stock portfolio? I've tried many different approaches, but always come back to covered calls.

Ron Clausen
Castro Valley, CA

I have read *Show Me the Money* and refer to it often. His Visions software is extremely helpful in picking the right stock, CC, or Put. Have made money using his methods and materials. His new books I'm sure will be very insightful.

Maurie Deming
Roswell, Georgia

Ron's system has helped me get over the "oh no the market is down, I am losing money" attitude. Now I can make money in a down market or an up market. Thank you Ron.

Don Featherston
Dallas, TX

Ron's earlier books started me on a consistent and profitable path that unlocked the hidden value in my current and helped with my choice of future stocks in my 401K. These methods and evaluation techniques can provide market beating returns on a monthly basis. I have used these over the years with very satisfyingly consistent results. I am now confident of where my supplemental retirement income needs will come from. Thanks Ron!!!

Steve Friis
North Fond du Lac, WI

I have used Visions for over 3 years and have been to two seminars in Florida.

I cut my teeth with monthly options using Visions.

About a year ago I got into weekly and Ron adapted Visions to help me find the right option.

I do monthly and weekly options and average over 1% a week return on money invested.

Visions helps me do this and The Trade Planner helps me organize the plan.

Best to all.

Jim Gantt
Albemarle, NC

What I like about Ron Groenke:

He was a programmer first and then became an investor. That meant that he could program his own ideas so they work on a computer. Where else can you find that? On top of that, he really cares about his clients. If you have a problem or question, shoot him an email or call him. If he doesn't answer the phone, his wife will. His books are easy to read and understand and his seminars are a "charm." This is before you even get to the heart of the matter—how an average person can make money using covered calls.

Regards,

Skip Gantt
NC

Since I retired about 4 years ago, the stock market has been my major source of income. If I depended on my Social Security check to survive, we'd starve. I've tried some of everything...trading futures, Forex, LEAPS, stocks/ETFs ... but I can truly say that the majority of my profits have come from covered calls and naked puts. Ron's book (from the 1st one through the later revisions) and his seminar have played a HUGE part of my success. I have given a number of copies to some of my trading buddies because I think it has so much to offer toward their success. I endorsed the last version, *Show Me the Money*, and its predecessor, *Cash for Life*, and I am confident this new book will contribute to my future continued success as well. I can't wait to get my hands on it.

Richard Goudeau
Macon, GA

Ron Groenke's book *Show Me The Money* showed me that trading options can be done profitably while minimizing risk. But with no previous options trading experience I decided to attend an upcoming Seminar to learn more. Ron is an excellent teacher and answered all our questions clearly. That experience gave me the confidence to open a new investment account using only the "Visions" software to pick the stocks best suited for options trading. In the three years that I have been using the software, my "Visions" account has averaged 26% return per year.

Thank You Ron,

Andy Guti
Naples, FL

Life is a continual learning process. Isn't that true of investing? So why shouldn't I continue to learn more about making smart investing trades?

Like all the previous Groenke's books and Visions software investment tools, *Show Me the Trade* promises to be another entertaining and very informative resource. It too, will certainly help me profitably trade with more expertise in the stock and options market to produce monthly cash income as planned.

Conrad Haas
Suffolk, VA

Ron's proprietary technical analysis method (VTAM) is the real deal based on the price behavior of each stock or fund over time. In simple terms, VTAM helps you to "buy low" and sell "higher." I've made good money consistently using VTAM.

George V. Hartmann
Stockton, CA

I have been using Ron's Visions software for two years now. It gives me two of the things that I lack… discipline and a consistent frame of reference. I read widely in the financial press, and am often tempted by the latest hyped "wunder-stock." I do not even consider the stock that is being touted until I have run it through the Visions program.

All the best,

Jason Hicks
Denver, CO

Thanks for the opportunity to comment on the seminar I attended in Naples, FL back in 2009.

Ron's seminar on covered calls was thorough, enlightening and together with his website and software, proved to be very profitable.

I would also highly recommend Ron's books which will give you an insight into the world of option trading. When I had a question to ask, Ron was always very prompt in answering and offering a solution via email.

Chris Holmes
Austin, TX

In my opinion, Ron's books, software and seminar are aimed to all levels of investors. The books are very readable and not full of 'proprietary' buzz words used to rename common trading vehicles. The material is a very very good value when compared to 'systems' costing thousands of dollars. With Ron's system you don't have to buy very expensive add-ons. There is no need to pay a monthly fee for 'extra' software. Someone looking for value, usability and great support should give Ron's system very serious consideration.

Dave Hurst

Ron is an educator. He is teaching people how to fish. I think he is doing a great job. I have gotten a great education reading his books and following VISIONS software. Keep up the good work!

John Jefferies
Williamstown, NJ

Ron's books should be read by anyone seeking personal control of their own financial resources. The emphasis of Ron's book series is income generation through safe and predictable selling of option contracts. Market and transaction understanding and strategy is conveyed through simple conversational story lines. The mechanics and the process of finding and executing a profitable trade are well-described. I have profitably used these income generation processes on regular stock accounts and on IRAs. Ron's VISIONS software provides several tools to quickly and effectively search out, evaluate, and execute Ron's strategy for income generation.

Dave Loomis
Retired management-type
Minneapolis, MN

Ron's seminar captures what is in the books in his online system and he willingly answers questions. The seminar is fast paced but Ron makes sure you understand what's going on by answering questions in the class and during breaks.

Royce Lyles
The Villages, FL.

After a decade of flat returns, my account has grown by 50% in 2012 with Ron Groenke's help.

Ted Kellis

Read Ron's book in 2008 and started trading covered calls at that time. Have had excellent returns exceeding my goal of 15% annualized ROI.

Have found the "Visions" program a superior program for researching the best values for option results.

Would recommend Ron's book for any who want to learn how to gain better results and handle their own investments successfully.

Best always

Tom Lupfer
Waco, Texas

I have read all of Ron Groenke's books, attended his seminar and subscribed to his trading plan. Ron's system is straight forward and easy to understand. More importantly, Ron updates the system as needed and uses the system for his trading and posts the results of his trading on the website. If you want to trade covered calls, this is the best system I have found.

Royce Lyles
Gainesville, FL

Ron's books have taken a trading strategy that is complex to most people (selling covered calls and naked puts) and made it very easy to understand, implement, and be profitable with. I would recommend Ron's books to anyone that manages their own portfolio or is considering managing their own portfolio.

Best regards,

Troy Mason

I got a copy of *Show Me The Money* last year and only wish I had found it sooner.

I had been picking stocks and waiting for appreciation before I got *Show Me The Money*. What a mistake that was, for me anyway!

I read your book, tried the trial software and immediately purchased it after the trial period was up. And guess what, I purchased it with cash I made using the trial software!

Your fundamental ideas about using options, to add your portfolio, are great!

On rare occasions I do get into trouble by thinking the old way, ignoring your philosophy, and buy a stock with the hopes that it will zoom through the roof. Of course that rarely happens and has not worked for me yet.

I have been hitting singles and doubles since using your method and have been consistently adding money to my trading account. I only wish I had found it sooner.

I am looking forward to getting your new book, *Show Me the Trade*, when it becomes available, to continue to add to my retirement "nest egg!"

Thank you,

Bill McCarthy

Hello. I've very much enjoyed *Show Me the Money* since it keeps me on the right side of my trades thus allowing me to supplement my retirement income by selling puts.

Thanks

Gus McClay
Springfield, Pa

I've been successfully trading in the options markets for ten years. Although I was doing well it wasn't until I read Ron's book, *The Money Tree*, that I really began to make money consistently. I then read, *Show Me the Money* and attended one of Ron's two day seminars. They strongly reinforced my money management skills. Ron has mastered the covered call and cash secured put area of trading and is able to impart his skills to others very readily. I wholeheartedly endorse this new book and hope everyone benefits from Ron's work as well as I have.

Bob Milota
Gainesville, FL

I have been following Ron's approach to covered call and naked put trading and using his VISIONS software since July 2008. I have found that it greatly enhances my success in finding winning trades. Having previously tried multiple other approaches to trading covered calls and naked puts I have found Ron's system produces far better results with less risk.

Regards,

Troy Mills
Flower Mound, TX

Ron certainly has the right combination of knowledge, not only from his computer background, but also from his passion for the market. Put the two together, and it can be lethal information. Thanks Ron.

Russ Morris,
Seminole, Florida

I love Ron's books. They are full of information that's presented in an easy-to-understand format.

As a result of what I've learned from Ron, several of my friends have joined to sell covered calls. I'm getting ready to make the big jump to retirement and without Ron's knowledge and practice it wouldn't even be a possibility.

Best regards,

Mary Moss
Milwaukee, Wisconsin

I have attended two of Ron's workshops, and read all his books (at least twice). My experience has been that Ron's VISIONS programs have produced the best consistent returns than any other "system" I have ever used during my 50 year business career. My profits on invested capital average between 1.0 % & 2%+ every month, pretty much regardless of market action. I strongly urge investors to learn how to select and "rent" stocks for a great return with minimal risk—VISIONS has made my retirement financially satisfying with a minimum of risk and effort, and it is easy to learn!

Arthur P. Mullin CCIM , MBA
Scottsdale, AZ

I have been trying to invest in the market for past 10 years with net loss every year. Only after I read Ron's book, *Show Me the Money* and used Visions software, I was able to double my 70K in investments to 140K in a matter of 2 years. The concept is enlightening.

It is a great tool and even though it is intended for the retirement age I went ahead and used it in my 40's and was able to gain. This book should be read by every investor.

Kudos to Ron for creating such a great software and an awesome book.

Gautam Patel
Plainsboro, NJ

After reading all of Ron's books and taking a class from him, I am deeply appreciative for the simple, clear and precise method that he teaches to trading. I have read over 30 books on trading, and Ron's is one of the simplest and most enjoyable reads. After thousands of trades, I am still using his methods and I find that they produce consistent profits. His software is very easy to use and understand. It saves me a lot of time and is fun. Thank you Ron!

Thank you for the opportunity!

Randy Perez
Columbus, GA

I thought I knew everything about investing until I heard of Ron. With the visions software I was able to turn my portfolio around even in a down market!! It's been less work on me to invest and more money in my pocket. How can you go wrong with that? Thank you so much Ron for finally making me a truly wise investor.

Amanda Sauls

I think I can truly say that Ron's books and his Vision's software have given me the tools and confidence to move forward successfully on selling options. It was critical in these economic times for me to find a reliable source of income through investing. And Ron's seminar was extremely worthwhile because of the "one on one" support and explanations of the software and trading philosophy.

I can't thank him enough for his support and encouragement.

Karen Sausman
Mountain Center, California

Ron's books provide a very concise trading methodology, when followed produces mostly favorable trading results. Of course no trading methodology is for sure, you certainly have a winning chance with this system. Ron also supports you with his personal email address. He personally answers your questions in a timely manner. I look forward to be able to attend one of his seminars. I know I will learn more valuable insights about trading.

    Thank you Ron,

Florence Shaw
Albany, NY

Show Me the Money is a must for somebody who wants enjoy life and make money. Easy to read, easy to understand. If you don't know what covered calls are and how you can get cash flow month after month spending a couple minutes a day it will be change your financial health right away!

Joe Shmukler

I have been using Visions for over two years and the Show Me the Money Trade is a great Tool and Resource when you need unbiased analysis on when to buy, hold or sell. Ron's Black Box VTAM program is one of the best products on the market for trading stocks and options!!!!

Steven Siegel
Westbury, NY

The seminar was well organized and highly informative. The practice sessions helped make the learning stick. It was a great investment and time well spent. I recommend completely.

Dean Slack
Westport, CT

I thank Ron for helping me, through his books and also the Visions programme, to the point where I now make my own decisions.

    I highly recommend the seminar, I gained tremendous knowledge and direction through the course. All this has helped me be able to retire by the end of this year.

    Thanks Ron.

Cameron Smith
Ontario, Canada.

The Ron Groenke seminar gives a good overview of all the functionality of the Visions software. Ron is always improving on and adding new features to the Visions software. In the seminar, Ron explains the purpose of each feature and goes through examples using the feature. You gain a complete understanding of the software. This maximizes your ability to use the software, so you can decide which components will help you the most in making your investment decisions. Ron also takes you through an actual investment cycle. He uses the Visions software to find a stock, explaining the reasoning behind his choice. He then actually buys the stock in the class. You can see how the Visions software can be utilized for your own investment strategies. You tend to not use portions of software that you do not understand. The seminar will provide that knowledge, so you can get the greatest benefit from the Visions software.

Denise Stein
Atlanta, Georgia

I attended the Feb 2011 seminar, well worth the price! Ron covered the Visions system from A to Z and explained in layman's language how to understand the market and use Visions to reap profits. Unlike other seminars I've attended, Ron wasn't trying to sell anything; his goal was to make sure all in attendance understood the power of Visions. In a short time I had more than covered the seminar cost with profits. After many years of research, I finally have a system that works as advertised.

Tommy Thomasson
Carrollton, GA

I was lucky enough to find one of Ron's books (*Covered Calls and Naked Puts*) at the local library on the Air Force Base back in November 2011. Since reading that book, which was an older version, I then bought his more recent book, *Show Me the Money,* which was the newer version of the same book, and also purchased all his software programs in December 2011 and put them into place to start investing. I started my portfolio off with $23,500 and in just the first 2 months I have earned $7,568 in profits for an estimated annual return of nearly 193%.

I have read a lot of different investment books, all of which were boring and nearly the same type of stuff, but Ron's books were *quite* easy to read and were easy to implement the strategies. I am so thankful that someone was nice enough to place one of his books in the library for me to discover!! I look forward to reading all his future books and using his software for years to come!!

John Wallace
Anthem, AZ

I am looking forward to Ron's new book. After reading Ron's last two books I have greatly improved my investment performance. One stock I own is down in price from when I purchased it over a year ago but by using Ron's methods I am actually up in my total investment. What a great system, one that allows you to make money even when the stock you bought long may be down from your original entry point.

Thanks Ron and keep up the great work.

Paul Wilken

I am retired and interested in generating additional income. *Show Me the Money* got me excited about Ron's approach, and his seminar was well planned, well presented, and extremely helpful in getting started with his VISIONS software. I value the fact that with VISIONS Ron is sharing the tools of his own investing, not just marketing a clever product. He continues to improve and develop the package, actively communicates to users with news and announcements, and is interested in our success. Dividing my time between Maine and Florida, I love being able to run VISIONS anywhere—all I need is a laptop and Internet access. This is a great tool that I intend to use for a long time.

Lanny Carroll
Naples, FL and Scarborough, ME

Disclaimer

There is a high degree of financial risk when trading in the stock and options market. The author and publisher stress that it is possible to lose money that is invested in these markets. The methods and techniques presented in this book may be profitable or they may result in a loss. Past results are not necessarily indicative of future results. The examples of specific companies that are used in this book are only for informational purposes and are not recommendations.

This publication is sold with the understanding that the author and publisher are not engaged in providing legal, accounting, or other professional services. If legal advice or other expert assistance is required, the services of a competent professional should be sought. Although every precaution has been take n in the preparation of this book, the publisher and author assume no liability for errors and omissions. This book is published without warranty of any kind, either expressed or implied. Furthermore, neither the author nor the publisher shall be liable for any damages, either directly or indirectly arising from the use or misuse of the book.

Before investing, learn as much as you can about the investments that you plan to make. Do extensive research. Knowledge will put the odds in your favor.